W9-CSP-715

GOOD NEWS By FRANCES EASTMAN

UNITED CHURCH PRESS   BOSTON, PHILADELPHIA

New Printing, 1966

Copyright © 1964 by the United Church Press. Printed in the United States of America. All rights reserved. No part of the text or illustrations may be reproduced in any form without written permission of the publishers, except brief quotations used in connection with reviews in magazines or newspapers.

The scripture quotations in this publication are from the *Revised Standard Version of the Bible,* copyrighted 1946 and 1952 by the Division of Christian Education, National Council of Churches, and used by permission.

This book is part of the United Church Curriculum, prepared and published by the Division of Christian Education and the Division of Publication of the United Church Board for Homeland Ministries.

Library of Congress Catalogue Card Number 64-14496

CONTENTS

OUR STORY

WHAT'S IT ALL ABOUT?

Bob leaned against the arched doorway of the chapel. Absent-mindedly he scuffed one foot in the dirt, juggled two rocks in one hand, and jingled the coins in his pocket with the other.

"Sure wish the reverend would hurry up and get here," he remarked. "I'd like to get through this rehearsal in time to play softball."

"I'd just like to get through the rehearsal, period," replied Bill from his post on the stone fence surrounding the chapel area. "Why did they have to pick me to help serve communion anyway? If I've got to pass something, the offering plates would suit me a lot better."

"Why?" asked Nancy. "What's the difference between passing the bread plates and the offering plates?"

Bill looked at Nancy in amazement. "Don't you use what's inside that head of yours for anything?" he inquired sarcastically. "What's the difference, she wants to know!" he scoffed, turning to Bob. "Think, girl, think!" he continued, favoring Nancy with a lofty look that couldn't quite mask the expression of mingled distaste and discomfort lurking in his eyes. "With the offering plates you're just taking up what people give to the conference offering. But in communion, well, put it this way. You're passing out bread that's supposed to be Jesus' body and grape juice that's his blood. I ask you, how queer can you get? And can you tell me what it's really all about? Just because people have been doing this forever and ever doesn't tell you what it's all about, does it?"

"Take it easy, old man," said Bob soothingly. "You don't want to get your temperature up too high. They might pop you in the infirmary, and that'd be worse than serving communion any day, wouldn't it?"

"Bob!" exclaimed Nancy reproachfully. "How can you be so crude? You sound positively irreverent, and communion's a very reverent matter. People are always quiet, and it sounds so noble as the minister reads. I've watched in church, and it seems so sort of hushed and dignified, even if I don't quite know all the words the minister reads, or what they mean. Sometimes I even want to cry when I think about Jesus dying."

"But Nancy!" exclaimed Bill, as Bob shook his head over the mystery of girls. "Doesn't it bother you that you don't know what the bread and grape juice are all about? How do they tie Jesus' death up to us? Oh, I know, this was his last meal before he was executed, but what's all this got to do with us? That's what I want to know!"

Bill's voice sounded as though his insides were all twisted up in trying to get the words out. His face looked that way, too.

Jeannette, who had been sitting beside Nancy without saying a word, looked up at him with a friendly nod of her curly, brown head. "You're really taking it hard, Bill," she said softly. "But I sort of know what you mean. I don't really know what it's all about either, but do you know how I feel?"

Bill shook his head, and Bob turned an interested eye in Jeannette's direction.

"I feel sort of guilty," added Jeannette, "and I don't know quite why. Sort of . . . oh . . . as though I shouldn't be taking communion, even though I've joined the church. It's as if I weren't worthy of all Jesus did. Somehow," she continued with a sudden burst of words, "it seems as though he did something wonderful for us when he died. He was so good and so brave, and he seemed to be trying to say something very special at that last supper. If I only knew what it was! I'd feel more worthy then. I know I would."

Nancy had been listening carefully as the conversation proceeded. "Jeannette," she announced, "you make me feel as though I ought to have thought more about communion. You and Bill both make me want to know more about it. I'm beginning to feel a little as Bill does: kind of edgy about passing out the bread and grape juice tonight. And always before I've thought it was so lovely and so moving and peaceful."

2

For a moment no one said a word. The only sound was the jingle of Bob's coins. "I wonder," he was thinking, "why I've never thought about communion." He had realized suddenly that he simply sat in the pew at the communion service and waited for the trays of bread and wine to be passed. At this point, try as he might, he couldn't remember what the minister had said about communion in church membership class. Something about the night Jesus died was all that Bob could recall. "Why do you suppose I've never tried to tie it up with me, as Bill and Jeannette do?" he wondered, almost guiltily.

Bob suddenly realized that a fifth person had joined the group. Henry Peterson, dean of the conference, was sitting at the end of the fence. Bob was so surprised that he dropped his stones.

"Reverend!" he exclaimed. "I didn't see you come!"

The three other young people whirled around at the sound of Bob's voice. "Reverend!" they echoed. "How long have you been here?"

"Mister Peterson, if you please," the dean replied with a twinkle. "None of this reverend business. Haven't you heard?"

The four young people grinned. They had heard. Ministers were not supposed to be addressed as reverend without benefit of their full names, but it was fun to call Dean Peterson that anyway, and he was a good sport about it.

"I've been here for the last several paragraphs of your conversation," the dean continued more seriously.

"You *have?*" The four conversationalists looked startled. They glanced at one another guiltily, wondering what the dean would think about the things they'd said about communion.

The dean seemed to read their thoughts. "I'm glad you felt you could say what you did," he remarked. "Communion must seem a very strange and mysterious custom. There's nothing like it in any of your other experiences, is there? It is a sacrament, you know. That is, it's a visible sign or symbol of an inner, spiritual reality we feel deeply but cannot see. Perhaps you've heard that before?"

Four faces frowned as their owners tried to follow the dean's meaning.

He smiled. "Well, let me try to put it another way. Communion stands for our sharing, through Jesus Christ, in the love God gives us so freely if we're willing to receive it and love him in return. And it is God's love that is the real source of life for us."

Looks of slight relief passed across the faces of the four listeners, but the puzzled expressions were not erased entirely. Once more the dean smiled. "I see we're making a little progress," he remarked, and looked thoughtfully toward the cross on the chapel.

"I've got it!" he exclaimed, snapping his fingers joyfully. "I'll try to write it down in a story. No, not a kid's story," he added hastily as he read the faces of his audience once more. "This will be *our* story."

"*Our* story?" inquired Bill. "Whadaya mean? About this conference?"

Dean Peterson shook his head and nodded it, all at once. "Yes, about us here at the conference, or us back in our home churches, or us anywhere Christians are found in the whole world! You see," he added earnestly, "the story of how God makes his love known to us really began a long time ago when he first created man to live on this earth. God has used a very special way to make his love known to human beings. He has done it by coming into their lives, into history, we might say. He has acted through people, most supremely through the life, death, and resurrection of Jesus Christ. The communion service we will share tonight is an occasion when we celebrate again his living presence among us and remember how greatly, acting through Christ, God loves us.

"This story is a wonderful piece of good news. It is the very heart of the Christian faith. It is one of the great unifying messages of the Bible. I think the story will help you understand what communion is, and why it is a sacred, reverent occasion." The dean looked understandingly at Nancy. "One that we're really not worthy of." He glanced at Jeannette with a brief smile. "And yet one that brings us to God and his love." The dean nodded at Bill. With a glance at Bob he added, "And one we need to think about and take very seriously."

Here is the story the dean wrote down for the four deacons and their friends.

Ramses II, probable pharaoh of the exodus, Luxor, Egypt

FREEDOM! PRAISE GOD!

Based on Exodus 12:29–39; 13:17—14:31; and 15:19–21

The news spread quickly among the slaves. Even under the watchful eyes and snapping whips of Egyptian overseers the word was passed along.

A man named Moses had appeared, seemingly out of nowhere, with the news that God would deliver the people from their bondage. No one believed him at first. After all, who was he? Years ago, some of the elders recalled, he had been a prince in the household of Pharaoh. Then one day he had killed an Egyptian overseer for beating a Hebrew slave. After that no one had heard anything further about him. He had run for his life, no doubt. The pharaoh would deal harshly with a member of his own household who had taken sides with the Hebrews and killed one of the king's own retainers for beating a slave.

But here he was again, fresh from the wilderness. There, so he and his brother announced, Yahweh (yä′ wĕ),* who was the God of the Hebrews, had met him with the command to come back to Egypt and lead the slaves into freedom!

The people shook their heads in unbelief at such news when it first trickled through the Hebrew settlement in the Nile delta. Yahweh, *their* God? They scarcely knew who their God was. Now why would he suddenly take such an interest in them and their meager existence? It was unbelievable.

When days passed and the work orders grew even harsher—to go out and find their own straw for making bricks, yet keep up the same production quota every day—resentment began to smolder among the slaves. This man Moses had brought this upon them, they learned from their elders. He had told Pharaoh to let the people go so they could take a three-day trip into the wilderness to worship. Naturally the king had been suspicious. The harsher work orders had resulted, with the overseers more cruel than ever. The slaves groaned and began to plot how they could get rid of this man Moses for good.

But then a new tale spread through the settlement. Moses had appeared before Pharaoh again. "Let my people go!" was what he had told the king. This was a command, not from him, but from the LORD their God. Pharaoh was as stubborn as ever, but strange things were happening. More devastating plagues of gnats and flies than usual swarmed upon the Egyptians—but not on the Hebrews. Locusts were devouring the Egyptian crops; cattle were dying; hail and darkness were covering the land. Yet the Hebrews' little corner of the delta region seemed untouched. Were all these weird events the work of the God whom Moses was representing? *Their* God? Awe and a touch of fear crept into the slaves. What

---

* Yahweh is the English translation of YHWH, the Hebrew name for God. In the King James and the Revised Standard versions of the Bible this word is translated LORD (printed in capitals). This book will use the proper name Yahweh at some points and LORD at others in referring to the God of Israel.

would be the outcome of all this? No one on earth was mightier than Pharaoh. Look at the huge columns of the temple they were building for him, the enormous statues they were erecting. His word was law. Could Yahweh their God prevail against Pharaoh? Hope began to edge quietly into the news that was reported day by day across the fields and at the brick pits. Pharaoh had not let them go, but there was a strange sense that mighty things were happening.

Then came the great news, the news the people had been waiting for without quite realizing it. The hour had come! Every man worked hard that day. Passive faces looked back blankly when the overseers uttered their usual curses. Backs trembled beneath strokes of the lash, but the spirit of the workers was different. Moses had told the people to prepare to go. That very night the LORD would pass over Egypt and deliver them to freedom.

Freedom? What was that? The people did not know. For several hundred years they had been slaves. Once an ancestor, Joseph, had been a royal official in Egypt, but hard times had come after his services were forgotten. No one knew what freedom was, except that it would mean no more of Pharaoh's forced labor, no more of the overseers' cruel beatings. Their God would watch over them. He had sent Moses to be their leader. The people trusted Moses now. There was nothing else they could do. Why not pack up and go? What had they to lose?

Every lintel and doorpost in the Hebrew camp was splattered with the blood of a lamb that night. It was a sign to the LORD, Moses had said. He would keep that house from harm as he passed over Egypt to do the final mighty deed that would make Pharaoh let the people go. Everyone remembered the solemn injunction Moses had added to his instructions:

> "And when you come to the land which the LORD will give you, as he has promised, you shall keep this service. And when your children say to you, 'What do you mean by this service?' you shall say, 'It is the sacrifice of the LORD's passover, for he passed over the houses of the people of Israel in Egypt, when he slew the Egyptians but spared our houses.'"

—Exodus 12:25–27a

No one could forget the commanding figure of Moses as he had pronounced those words. There he stood, arm outstretched, fire blazing deep in his eyes, and a ring of authority in his voice that was utterly different from the harsh grunts and bellows of the Egyptian overseers. This man was speaking for God. Every man, woman, and child fell to his knees and bowed his head. The Hebrews' God was mightier than they had ever imagined. Let him lead them on to freedom and to a new land of their own!

Shortly after midnight the word came. Their God had acted. Death had entered every Egyptian household. Unbelievable? Yes, but Pharaoh had at last told Moses to get the people and all their flocks and herds out of the country. The Egyptians were begging them to leave now. Their God had delivered them. What a mighty, mighty God this Yahweh must be!

No time was lost. Eastward across the delta region the people streamed. Cattle and sheep, women and children, young men and old men—all were there, trudging across the sand flats toward the swampy marshes which ran northward from the Red Sea and divided the plains of the delta from the rocky wilderness to the east. The first evening they made camp at the edge of the marsh.

There the several thousand escaping slaves tried to straighten out their families and their possessions and get a little rest after the wild escape. Never before had they been on their own.

As the people looked back that first night, their dismal homes in the delta began to seem comfortable. Camping in the open was frightening, with the vastness of the skies stretching out above them and the unknown marshes lying before them. Their little stores of food suddenly began to seem small indeed in the face of the need of many days of traveling. The people were glad to see the dawn drive away the night's eerie shadows. But the day brought its own terrors. In the morning when the people looked around, they saw behind them the Egyptian army in pursuit.

A wail of fear and anger surged over the encampment. Moses! Where was Moses? He had brought this upon them! He had persuaded them to escape. Better to have died in Egypt than to be killed by Pharaoh's soldiers in the middle of this wasteland of reeds and water. Where now was the LORD who would deliver them?

Moses was equal to the occasion. He summoned the people to gather around him. "Don't be afraid," he said, and the same fire burned in his eyes, the same authority rang in his voice. "The LORD your God will save you, as he already has saved you. Be quiet; have courage; trust the LORD. He will fight for you."

Wonderingly, the slaves obeyed this new master. The rest of that day and all night they waited. The Egyptians did not attack. In the early morning the wind came up from the east. A path of dry land was found through the waters of the marshland. Orderly and calm, the Hebrews followed their leader across. They looked back. The Egyptians had started to follow. Mud was clogging their heavy chariot wheels. The wind was now blowing from another direction, and the waters of the swamp were covering up the pathway of dry land and the armies on it.

Could it be? Could it be? The Egyptians overwhelmed in the middle of the very land the Hebrews had just walked through? The Hebrews could scarcely believe what they saw.

"The LORD has done this!" someone exclaimed. "Only the LORD could have saved us from the Egyptians!"

"The LORD!" everyone began to exclaim. "Yahweh is the Lord our God. He has done this for us. He has saved us. We are free!"

With a great shout the whole camp began to sing for joy. Never had there been such cause for rejoicing. There simply never had been a day like this in their lifetimes, or their fathers' lifetimes, or their fathers' fathers' lifetimes! This God whom they hardly knew had heard their cries and groanings and had delivered them from their oppressors. The mighty Pharaoh had gone down into the dirt before this God who had taken pity on his people.

"Sing to the LORD," chanted Miriam, sister of Moses, as she clapped her timbrel and danced ecstatically before the camp.

"Sing to the LORD," chanted the women as they followed her, clapping their timbrels and swirling their veils to the rhythm of the dance.

> "Sing to the LORD, for he has triumphed gloriously;
> the horse and his rider he has thrown into the sea."
> —*Exodus 15:21*

God had saved the Hebrews.

"ALL THAT THE LORD HAS SPOKEN"

Mount Sinai

Based on Exodus 19:1–15; 20:1–17; and 24:3–8

Travel through the wilderness was rough going. The sun burned down mercilessly by day. The chill air of the night found the people shivering and huddling together in tents for warmth. In Egypt they had had their little shelters; they had known where they would be. And food! Ah, they had eaten bread to their fill back in the delta land. Water? They had not suffered from thirst in the abundance of Egypt. But life in the wilderness was another matter. There was no food to which they were accustomed, almost no water, and when they did find some in a straggling little oasis it was often bitter, worse than none at all.

Day by day the memories of Egypt, with its warmth and regular provisions, grew rosier and rosier. The people railed bitterly at Moses. "Why didn't we die in Egypt, where we could at least eat our fill and quench our thirst? Now we will perish here in this wilderness. Why have you brought us here to die?"

The rugged stone mountains of the wilderness and the rough graveled plains were a new and terrifying world for the Hebrews. Never before had they been compelled to look out for themselves. In a new country they hadn't the faintest notion of what to do.

Moses stood between them and disaster like one of the great rocks they saw every day. From his years of herding sheep in this forbidding country, he had learned how to sweeten water with a certain tree, or strike the thin shell-like rock surface of a stone and find sweet water gushing below. The flight of quails was no secret to him. The art of gathering flake-like manna as it congealed from certain bushes was also one of his skills.

Patiently Moses met the complaints and abuse of the people. When a crisis arose he produced water, or manna, or quail. Once, when the whining cries of thirst had changed into threats, Moses almost despaired, and cried out to God: "What shall I do with this people? They are almost ready to stone me!" (Exodus 17:4)

Yahweh responded, supporting Moses as he supported the helpless people. Water was found, and the march through the wilderness continued. That strange sense of mighty things happening crept over the people again. They saw that Moses depended on God. From his mighty hand came food and water and victory in battle against hostile tribes who tried to block their march. Behind Moses, the people sensed the presence of their God, leading them on their way.

Three months after their escape, they made camp before a towering mountain. A story spread quickly from tent to tent. It was on this very mountain that God had met Moses and sent him

11

back to free the people. This was the spot to which Moses had been leading them all the time. What would happen now? What were they here for?

The call to assemble brought a quiver of expectation, and all the people gathered before Moses.

"You have seen what Yahweh, your God, did to the Egyptians, haven't you?" he announced.

"Yes!" shouted the people.

"And you have seen how the LORD has led you here, providing for your needs even when you doubted and would have turned back?"

The people nodded their assent.

Moses seemed to stand taller than ever as he went on speaking. "Now, therefore, if you will obey the LORD and keep the covenant which he is about to give you, you will be to him a holy nation, a people who will serve him with your whole lives. Will you obey his voice and keep his covenant?"

The people looked at one another, nodding their heads. The God who had saved them was graciously giving them assurance of his continuing favor. Of course they would agree to whatever conditions he required—and they would seal the promise with blood, as was the custom of their day.

With a great shout they replied, "All that the LORD has spoken we will do."

Two days of preparation for the ceremony followed. Garments were washed. Rituals of consecration were attended to. In great awe the people gazed at the mountain. It was a sacred spot, so holy that they dared not go near it or touch it. Only Moses might go up on it to meet God and talk with him. God was too mighty, too holy, for men to approach. Even Moses could not see him face to face.

On the morning of the day the covenant was to be given, Moses built an altar at the foot of the mountain. A stone pillar represented each tribe of the people. Oxen were killed as offerings to the LORD. The blood of the oxen was poured into containers. Moses took one basin holding half the blood and raised it high above his head. He dashed the blood against the altar.

A murmur of awe went up. This act signified the life-giving presence of the LORD in their midst. In the blood flowed life.

"Hear, O Israel," cried Moses, "what the LORD requires of you if you will keep his covenant and be his people. Hear the word of the LORD.

"I am the LORD your God, who brought you out of the land of Egypt, out of the house of bondage.
"You shall have no other gods before me.
"You shall not make yourself a graven image.
"You shall not take the name of the LORD your God in vain.
"Remember the sabbath day, to keep it holy.
"Honor your father and your mother.
"You shall not kill.
"You shall not commit adultery.
"You shall not steal.
"You shall not bear false witness against your neighbor.
"You shall not covet your neighbor's house."

—Exodus 20:2–17, passim

There was silence when Moses stopped. God had spoken plainly. He had left no doubt about what the people must do if they were to be his people and continue to enjoy his guidance and his saving help. His word had been spoken; his power had come among them. The people trembled and looked up at the great mountain and at the man who loomed before them almost as mighty as the mountain.

They bowed their heads. "All that the LORD has spoken we will do, and we will be obedient," they said.

Moses raised another basin containing the other half of the sacrificial blood. "Look!" he shouted, and threw the blood upon the people. "Behold the blood of the covenant which the LORD has made with you in accordance with all these words. He will be your God and you shall be his people."

The entire company fell upon its knees, heads bowed to the ground. The covenant had been sealed in blood. God's life had entered into theirs, and theirs had entered into his. He had given the covenant; they had received it. God and people were bound together. Thanks be to the God who had saved them and given them this new life under his care!

"CHOOSE YOU THIS DAY"

Based on Numbers 13:17—14:25 and Joshua 24:1—28

When the Hebrews said, "We will be obedient," they meant it, but they had little idea what they were saying. It took them a generation or more to find out. Life in the wilderness was full of problems. They were free—free to wander from oasis to oasis in the nomadic life they had exchanged for their secure but hopeless existence as slaves in Egypt. But freedom brought responsibilities. They had to learn how to find food and to defend themselves against other tribes who resented their intrusion into the wilderness territory.

Now and then some man was sure he could do a better job than Moses, and rebellion undermined the feeble sense of brotherhood that was painfully being born among the Israelites.

The same old cries of "Why did you bring us to die in this wilderness?" went up as Moses tried to lead this motley assortment of ex-slaves toward a permanent home in the land of Canaan to the north. Once they were in a position to advance into it from the south. Spies were sent ahead to see what the land and its inhabitants were like. They came back bearing huge clusters of grapes, ripe pomegranates, and figs.

Shechem Pass, Mount Gerizim on the left, Mount Ebal on the right

"It is a land flowing with milk and honey!" they reported to the hungry people. Visions of plenty to eat and rest from wandering at last filled the hearts of the weary Israelites. "But," added the spies, "the people are as big as giants. We can never make it!"

Two men, Caleb and Joshua, disagreed. "We can overcome them," they said.

But the damage had been done. "Let's go back to Egypt!" the people said to one another. "Let's choose a new captain. Why should we die in this wilderness?"

"Don't rebel against the LORD!" cried Moses. "He will protect us! Do not fear these people. They have no power if our God is with us!" He pleaded with God not to be angry with this people who would not believe in him.

So the Israelites had to find another route to the Promised Land. They had to go around the eastern borders of the land of Canaan and fight their way through hostile tribes there. Year after year they wandered and fought. The generation that came out of Egypt did not live to see its kinsmen cross over the Jordan River into the new land.

During the years of nomadic living, only Moses and the sense that Yahweh was leading them really held the people together. Only their common allegiance to the God who had saved them helped them learn to live with one another in the brotherly way they had promised to follow.

In the tent of meeting Moses sat to hear disputes and decide the right and wrong of quarrels. The people knew that here Moses talked with God and then worked out the details of how the law given at the mountain would be applied to the people's problems. Day after day Moses decided who had kept the law and who had broken it. And the people began to find out what "We will be obedient" meant in their daily living.

The people believed that Yahweh their God lived in the heavens, mighty and powerful, but that he was also present among them. They knew this because of the ark. This sacred chest contained the written code they had promised to keep as their covenant vow of thankfulness to God. When Yahweh came down from the heavens to lead them, they believed that he was invisibly enthroned upon the ark. When the ark was carried on ahead to a new camping place, he rode upon it to guide the scouts. When the ark rested in the middle of the camp, Yahweh was there.

"Arise, O LORD, and let thy enemies be scattered; and let them that hate thee flee before thee," sang Moses whenever the ark was taken on a journey. When it rested, he chanted this prayer, "Return, O LORD, to the ten thousand thousands of Israel." (Numbers 10:35–36)

Through the years the Israelites came to believe in their God and to act as though they believed. They crossed the Jordan River and stormed the city of Jericho. They burst upon the settlements of the central hill country of Canaan with a wild fervor which took the area by surprise. A string of Canaanite cities fell before the fierce confidence of the nomadic invaders. In the far north a toehold was also gained, and a few tribes settled there. The Israelites were welcomed by some tribes related to them who were found already living in the hill country. A generation—forty years—after they had escaped from Egypt, the slave tribes became united enough to fight their way into a new homeland.

Joshua was their leader now. Moses had died on the other side of Jordan, the vista of the Promised Land spread out before his eyes.

When the invasion campaign was ended, Joshua, like Moses, called all the tribes together. They gathered at the city of Shechem (shĕk′ ĕm), one of the military strongholds which the Israelites had entered—welcomed, apparently, by its original inhabitants. Mount Gerizim (gĕr′ ĕ-zĭm) rose above the city on one side of the narrow pass where it was located, Mount Ebal (ē′ băl) on the other.

"Thus says the LORD, the God of Israel!" announced Joshua, and the people listened attentively. The mantle of Moses as leader and spokesman for God had fallen upon Joshua. Their God was addressing them whenever he spoke.

"I took your father Abraham, says the LORD, when he served other gods, and led him to the land of Canaan and made his offspring many. I gave him Isaac, and to Isaac I gave Jacob, and Jacob and his children went down to Egypt . . ."

The recital went on. Joshua recalled the history of this people under God, how he had made of them a people, and had brought them into this land. Here they could now live in cities which they had not built, and eat the fruit of vineyards and olive orchards which they had not planted.

"God has been merciful and gracious to you!" proclaimed Joshua. "What will you do in return? Fear the LORD, and serve him in sincerity and in faithfulness."

Joshua then turned to the Israelites' relatives, the tribes who already were living in Canaan. "And you," he commanded, "put away the gods which your fathers have served. Make covenant with the LORD, God of Israel, and serve him. This you must do if you would receive his blessing."

Joshua looked out over the whole assembly. "Choose you this day whom you will serve."

There was no doubting his word. A choice had to be made—for the Israelites, to renew the covenant; for the other tribes, to enter into it. Life depended on receiving the blessing of the LORD.

No one spoke. It was an awesome silence. Joshua pointed to his own tribe. "As for me and my house," he declared, "we will serve the LORD."

Some of the people finally responded, "We will serve Yahweh as well as the gods our fathers served."

"Never!" thundered Joshua. "You cannot serve Yahweh and serve other gods at the same time. Yahweh demands that you serve him and him only. Choose you this day whom you will serve!"

Once more silence, and then a great shout. "We will serve the LORD!"

"You are witnesses to what you have sworn!" cried Joshua.

"We are witnesses," replied all the tribes. "The LORD our God we will serve, and his voice we will obey."

"This, then, is the covenant you have made," announced Joshua. And he read laws and ordinances, the commands of God that were to govern their lives in the land of Canaan.

The people bowed their heads and said, "These things we will do."

A great stone was set up under a huge oak tree. "This is the sanctuary of the LORD," Joshua told the assembly, "and this stone is witness to the words that the LORD has spoken—words which you will obey."

Israel had renewed her covenant with God. New members also had been received into the covenant people. They all were bound together under God. After the ceremony ended, the tribes separated to the places where each group would live in their new homeland.

The "Oak of Abraham" near Hebron. At a tree like this Abraham built his altar

BY FAITH

Based on Genesis 12:1–7

Once Israel had settled down in Canaan the tribes applied themselves to gaining more extended victories over the Canaanite settlers and to adjusting themselves to a different way of life. In Egypt they had been slaves. In the wilderness they had been nomads wandering from oasis to oasis in search of grazing land and food. In Canaan they now had to learn to become farmers. They also had to get the upper hand over the sophisticated, highly cultured people who lived in the walled cities of the land as well as in the central highlands.

This task was to require several generations to accomplish. Each tribe settled in a different region, so that the Israelites came to be scattered the length and breadth of the country. Some even lived on the other side of the Jordan. Mutual loyalty to the God who had given them this new life was the only tie that linked them together.

Now that the Israelites had a present and a future, they began to ponder their past. Dim tribal memories of ancestors and of the

God they had served became clearer. The people began to see a special connection with three forefathers who had been nomads in this very land: Abraham, Isaac, and Jacob. Jacob's family had gone down to Egypt in one period of migration, and his son Joseph had served a pharaoh so well that he became a royal official. The Israelites—named after Jacob, or Israel—came to believe that it was no accident that had brought these families to the land they now called their own. God had led them there.

It had all begun back in Ur, in the land of the Chaldees to the east, in the time of Terah and his son Abraham. Other gods had been worshiped there. No one knew Yahweh. Terah moved his family northward from Ur to Haran on the arc of fertile soil that linked the great rivers of the east with the coastal lands of the west. There he had died. And there Yahweh had appeared to his son Abraham.

"Leave this country," Yahweh had said. "Leave all the members of your father's household. Leave everything and go to the land where I will lead you. I will make a great nation of you. I will bless you; I will give you the power of life and well-being. You will be a blessing and by you all the families of the earth will be blessed."

Abraham did as he was commanded. Strange as it may have seemed, without knowing where he was going, he trusted God, took his family, and left Haran. Abraham came to the very place where Joshua later rallied the people to renew the covenant: to Shechem. Under the oak of Moreh (mō′rĕ) Abraham built an altar, for the LORD had appeared to him again and said, "To your descendants I will give this land." Again Abraham believed, even though at that time he had no child to whom descendants might be born.

As the Israelites thought about these ancient memories, they began to understand how, by faith, Abraham had responded to God's promise. He had trusted the LORD, as Moses had told them they must trust the very God who had led Abraham to the Promised Land. What mighty deeds God had done! And he would do yet greater ones if they were faithful to him. This was the promise of the covenant.

20

Captives of Ramses III who threw back the Philistines c. 1175. The fourth from the left is a Philistine

"LONG LIVE THE KING!"

Based on 1 Samuel 4:1–11; 8:1–22; and 10:17–27

A summons had come to all Israel. For nearly two hundred years calls to battle had been going the rounds of all the tribes. When danger threatened, the leader of the beleaguered tribe sent word to all the others: Arise, people of the LORD! Come to the aid of your brothers. In the name of the LORD, God of hosts, come.

The Philistines were the enemy now. These people had come up to the highlands from their cities on the coastal plain. Assembled by the sons of Eli, the Israelites went out to meet them. The battle was fiercely fought, line against line. Israel lost. It was a terrible defeat.

The elders held a council meeting afterwards. Why had they lost? "Because the ark of the covenant is still in the sanctuary at Shiloh!" they exclaimed. "It is not here so that Yahweh himself may save us from the power of the enemies."

21

The ark was brought up from Shiloh (shī′ lō). When it came into Israel's battle camp great shouting filled the air. The Philistines heard the noise off in their own camp. They wondered why people who had just lost hundreds of men in battle were filling the air with such a joyful noise. A spy reported: The ark of the LORD has just come into their camp. At this news the Philistines trembled, but their leader stepped into the situation with a firm hand.

"Act like men, you Philistines!" he commanded. "Fight—or you will be slaves to the Hebrews, dealt with as mercilessly as we have treated them."

So the Philistines fought. Not only did they defeat the Israelites so severely that the men broke ranks and fled, but they even captured the ark of the covenant and carried it off as a spoil of war.

Never had such a disaster befallen the Israelites. Never since they crossed Jordan to invade Canaan had they been in such a desperate situation. Even the city of Shiloh and its sanctuary had been destroyed in the terrible battle. The tribes of Israel began to think that their tribal league with God as king was not strong enough to defend them against vigorous attacks any longer. They needed something more to bind them together. As the people looked at other nations they saw that these stronger nations all had kings. Did Israel need a king?

For twenty years or so the question was not publicly voiced. After the fall of Shiloh Samuel replaced Eli and began to judge Israel. Against him the Philistines began to lose their power. They returned the ark of the covenant after keeping it only seven months. Israel heard rumors that the Philistines were afraid of the ark because their god, Dagon (dā′-gŏn), had fallen on his face in front of it.

Year by year Samuel made his circuits to hear the problems and difficulties which the people faced. From Bethel (bĕth′ ĕl) to Gilgal (gĭl′ găl) to Mizpah (mĭz′ pà) he went, and then back again to his home at Ramah (rā′ mà). The people trusted Samuel as he interpreted the word of the LORD to them. There had been no one like him since Moses.

But Samuel grew old, and his sons proved to be dishonest. Who

Wall of the Jebusites, Jerusalem. The tower may have been built by David

would succeed him as judge and seer? Representatives from all the tribes came to see Samuel.

"Appoint a king to govern us like all the nations," they said.

"A king!" Samuel was angry. Without responding, he turned to God in prayer.

"It is not you that the people are rejecting, Samuel," came the word of the Lord. "It is I. Ever since I led them out of Egypt, these people have been fickle and unfaithful. This is just another instance of what they always have done. Give them their way, but warn them that a king will oppress them. They will cry out against him, and regret that they ever turned against the Lord their God."

Samuel warned the people. He described what a king would do to make life harder and crueler for them. The people refused to listen.

"We want a king!" they shouted. "We want to be like all the nations. We need a king to govern us and go out before us and fight our battles for us."

And so a king was chosen. On the day that Saul, the first king of Israel, was anointed, Samuel said to the people, "If both you and the king who reigns over you will follow the Lord, your God, it will be well. Serve the Lord with all your heart, and he will not cast away his people, for Yahweh has made you a people for himself."

After Saul came David, the greatest king ever to rule Israel. Winsome of spirit and brave of heart, David was a popular monarch. He defeated the Philistines once and for all. He brought all the tribes together under his rule. He even conquered the fortified Canaanite city of Jerusalem. High on the hills of the southern tribal land of Judah it stood like a crown. There David made his royal residence, but the city was to be more. The rocky ridge of Zion in the midst of it came to be the dwelling place of the Lord.

How did it become so? By bringing the ark of the covenant to Jerusalem. David himself and the best men of the nation went to escort the ark to the capital city. People crowded the roadway to greet the procession with the ark. They sang before the Lord, for was not Yahweh riding enthroned upon the ark? They made music with their lyres and harps, their tambourines and castanets and cymbals. Horns sounded joyfully, and David danced before the ark as it was drawn along the way. Yahweh, God of Israel, was coming to Jerusalem!

A tent had been pitched on the ridge of Zion to house the ark until a more suitable temple could be erected as the dwelling place of the Lord. The ark was set in its place, and David made offerings to God. Then he blessed the people in the name of the Lord and gave them gifts. They went to their homes, rejoicing that now their God was present among them. He would give health and plenty to the king, who would bestow it upon the people.

Israel had become a nation like other nations. It had a king and a capital. There was just one difference. In Israel, God was still the true king. The king who ruled from a throne in the capital city ruled in the name of the Lord. He was not himself proclaimed a god, as happened in the land of Egypt.

WHO IS LORD OF NATURE?

Based on 1 Kings 17:1–3; 18

"You shall have no other gods before me" was the first and most important covenant obligation the Hebrews had agreed to in the time of Moses. Joshua had warned the covenant people at Shechem that they could worship only one god. There could be no other.

But Israel's memory proved rather short. Not only had she wanted to be like other nations and have a king, when God was supposed to be her true ruler, but she could not resist the temptation to worship the Canaanite gods along with Yahweh. After all, when the people first arrived in Canaan, they knew nothing about farming. How to raise crops was a complete mystery to them. Their Canaanite neighbors depended upon Baal (bā′ ăl), god of fertility and the storm, for the rains that were so necessary to the crops. Worshiping Baal with sacred rituals and magic rites was the way they tried to ensure that nature's cycle would repeat itself each year.

Baal worship was attractive. Its rituals were easier to follow than Yahweh's stern requirements of brotherly concern and mutual aid. And what did Yahweh have to do with crops? He was the mighty God who led the Israelites in war, in conquest, and in their relations with one another. But according to the Canaanites, Baal ruled the realm of nature. Without realizing that they were breaking their first and most important covenant obligation, the Israelites began to worship Baal in his sphere and Yahweh in his.

Then Jezebel (jĕz′ ĕ-bĕl) came to the Northern Kingdom. There were now two nations of Israelites, for David's empire had not lasted long, only through the reign of his son Solomon. Civil war had broken out and the nation became two nations, Israel in the north and Judah in the south, each with its own royal house.

God El (father of Baal) on a lion, from
Amrit, Syria

Jezebel had come from Phoenicia to be the wife of Ahab (ā' hăb), king of northern Israel. She was a woman with a mind of her own, and a fanatical worshiper of Baal Melkart, greatest of the fertility gods. She would not tolerate worship of two gods in her husband's kingdom.

With Ahab's indulgent permission, Jezebel set up altars to Baal and persecuted Yahweh's followers wherever she could find them. His prophets were all but wiped out. The few who were not killed went into hiding. Yahweh worship seemed doomed.

Then came the great drought. Three years passed without rain. The pastures dried up. Famine spread throughout Israel. King Ahab was desperate. Even his royal stable had no grass for the mules and horses. He remembered the prophet Elijah, a spokesman for the LORD, God of Israel, who had appeared unexpectedly in the palace three years earlier. Dressed in the rough clothing of a man from the rugged country across the Jordan, he had stalked into the king's presence and thundered forth this startling warning:

"As the LORD the God of Israel lives, before whom I stand, there shall be neither dew nor rain these years, except by my word!"

Then Elijah had disappeared, leaving the stunned king to think about his announcement. It had occurred to Ahab that Elijah was trying to usurp rain-giving powers for Yahweh, but he had dismissed the prophet's warning from his mind. When the drought grew steadily worse, he remembered it.

"Find that man!" Ahab ordered his servants. Maybe Elijah could end the drought as he had said he could. Messengers scoured kingdoms to the north and east of Israel. Elijah was nowhere to be found. Ahab gave up. Despairingly he ordered Obadiah (ō' bà-dī'á), the chief of his household, to search in every valley for grass for the animals. Obadiah went out and returned with news that left Ahab trembling with fear and hope. Elijah had reappeared. He was coming to see Ahab that very day.

The king could not wait. He hurried out to meet the prophet. "Is it you, you troubler of Israel?" he called out as he saw the familiar giant of a man coming down the road.

"I have not troubled Israel," the prophet retorted. "You and your family have brought this trouble on Israel. You have forsaken the

27

commandments of the true God and worshiped the Baals. We shall see who is lord, Yahweh or Baal. Assemble all the people at Mount Carmel and bring all the prophets of Baal there at the same time."

It never occurred to Ahab not to obey Elijah. Without question the king of Israel followed the orders of the prophet of Yahweh. The time to decide had come. Who *was* the lord of nature? Who gave the rains? Who was to be Israel's true god?

What happened on Carmel was never erased from Israel's memory. The recital grew more colorful as the years passed, and the people looked back in wonder on the truth made plain to them there. Elijah had put it with appalling clarity as they gathered on the promontory overlooking the sea to the west. They had felt guilty and frightened as the craggy giant strode up to them and shouted forth his question:

"How long will you go limping between two different opinions? You can't worship two gods. If the LORD is God, follow him; but if Baal, then follow him. Make up your minds."

No one said a word. Then Elijah proposed a contest. He and the priests of Baal would each prepare an animal sacrifice, but would light no fire beneath it. Each in turn would then call upon his god to send fire to consume his sacrifice. The people readily agreed. They watched as the demonstration went on.

How Elijah taunted the priests of Baal! "What's the matter?" he cried, when fire failed to consume their sacrifice. "Is your god off on a trip? Or asleep? Wake him up!" For hours the scathing taunts continued. Baal seemed no god at all by the time Elijah had finished his derisive jibes.

Then Elijah uttered his prayer. "Let this people know that thou, O LORD, art God, and that thou hast turned their faithless hearts back to thee!"

When the fire blazed on Elijah's altar it seemed like the word of the LORD itself descending upon them in judgment.

"The LORD, he is God!" they screamed, falling on their faces in worship and in fear. "The LORD, he is God!"

Then the rain came. Elijah's witness was complete. Yahweh, not Baal, was lord of the rains and giver of life. He was lord of the lives of the people of Israel.

Canaanite ivory box from Megiddo. Amos scorned such luxury

"FOR THREE TRANSGRESSIONS . . . AND FOR FOUR"

Israel's problems of keeping the covenant were not permanently solved when Elijah demanded that the people choose between Yahweh and Baal. A hundred years later another prophet of Yahweh addressed the people of the Northern Kingdom. He spoke in the marketplace of the busy city of Bethel. Wealthy Israelites stopped in the round of their business transactions to listen. The high priest was there. Perhaps some of the downtrodden poor hung on the edges of the crowd to listen too. This man wore the robes of a shepherd. His accent placed him as a southerner, perhaps from the hill country of Judah.

"Thus says the Lord!" he began, using words familiar to the lips of all true spokesmen for God.

> "For three transgressions of Damascus,
>> and for four, . . .
>> I will break the bar of Damascus, . . .
>>> and the people of Syria shall go into exile. . . ."

The people nodded approvingly at this news. They would be delighted to see their archenemy to the north go down in defeat.

> "For three transgressions of Gaza,
>> and for four, . . .
>> the remnant of the Philistines shall perish," . . .
> "For three trangressions of Tyre,
>> and for four, I will not revoke the punishment."

> —*Amos 1:3–9*

The roll call of Israel's neighbors went on. Nation after nation was doomed, announced the prophet. The LORD would punish their cruelty and their wickedness. Their time was not far off. The mounting fury of the prophet's warnings sent excited chills through his audience. "I told you so!" the people were thinking. "They'll get what they deserve, and we . . . well, Yahweh is *our* God. The prosperity Israel enjoys now is a sign of his approval. We are his people; he is our God. No harm will come to us."

Even Judah, Israel's sister kingdom to the south, was to receive her just deserts. For having rejected the law of the LORD, Jerusalem would be destroyed. Those words brought a thrill of anticipation to the prophet's hearers. And then the blow fell.

Thus says the LORD:

> "For three transgressions of Israel,
>> and for four, I will not revoke the punishment;
> because they sell the righteous for silver,
>> and the needy for a pair of shoes—
> they that trample the head of the poor into the dust of the earth,
>> and turn aside the way of the afflicted; . . .
> Behold, I will press you down in your place,
>> as a cart full of sheaves presses down."

> —*Amos 2:6–13*

Drawing of ivory
fragment   from
Megiddo

On and on the indictment ran. Angry murmurs of protest rumbled through the crowd. People began to shake their fists in the air. Voices broke into shouts of "Go away! Go away!" How dared this prophet denounce Israel, the very people to whom he was speaking, the chosen of Yahweh whom the Lord had favored with wealth and prosperity and every token of success? What did this prophet mean by coming into this center of luxury and denouncing the people to their faces?

The prophet, Amos, was undisturbed by the hostile reception his words received. He spoke, not for himself, but for God. He could readily see the luxurious life of the Northern Kingdom, but God had called him also to look beneath the veneer of luxury and see the wretched conditions which existed there. In every way these conditions were violations of the covenant God had made with his people.

The idle rich lived in houses trimmed with ivory and lay on couches made of the same costly stuff. They ate the finest of foods and drank from silver bowls. They were entertained with the most exquisite music, and bathed with the finest oils. They offered the best sacrifices and sang loud songs of praise before the altars of Yahweh. But outside their fine summer and winter homes, the poor were ground into the dust. Injustice ruled in the courts; bribes were offered and freely accepted on every hand. The needy had no chance for fair consideration of the wrongs done to them. Evil ruled; the truth was abhorred, and he who spoke it, disdained. Israel was rotten to the core—and believed that she was pure! She considered her prosperity a sign of her goodness in God's sight; her wealth the means of her salvation. But Israel was wrong.

"I hate, I despise your feasts,
    and I take no delight in your solemn assemblies.
Even though you offer me your burnt offerings and cereal
        offerings,
    I will not accept them,
and the peace offerings of your fatted beasts
    I will not look upon.
Take away from me the noise of your songs;
    to the melody of your harps I will not listen.

> But let justice roll down like waters,
>> and righteousness like an everflowing stream."
>> —*Amos 5:21–24*

Amos looked beyond the borders of Israel and saw the power of an empire rising in the east. The Lord would use that growing power, Assyria, as his instrument to judge Israel and punish her sins. The day of the Lord would be darkness, and not light.

At first the Israelites were made angry and anxious by Amos' gloomy predictions. Amaziah (ăm' à-zī-à), chief priest of the royal sanctuary at Bethel, drove Amos out of the country. There was an uneasy sense that mighty deeds were taking place. Whether the people liked it or not, the presence of the Lord was keenly felt in the uncompromising person of this shepherd of Tekoa who looked upon God as lord of surrounding nations as well as of Israel.

But after a while things settled down. Israel's uneasy feeling that she had broken the covenant and alienated the Lord faded away. Prosperity continued. King Jeroboam II (jěr-ō-bō'ăm) ruled magnificently for forty years. Surely *that* was a token of divine approval. The rich continued to grow richer, and the poor, poorer. The smoke of fragrant sacrifices rose more thickly, while the worshipers waited impatiently for the sabbath to end, so that they could get back to their business dealings and their juggling of money values and balance weights.

Yet Amos' words were not forgotten. They were preserved on a scroll and in the memories of some of the people who remembered that Yahweh had brought Israel out of Egypt, had led them through the wilderness to this land, and had commanded them to keep the covenant:

> Seek good, and not evil,
>> that you may live;
> and so the Lord, the God of hosts, will be with you, . . .
> Hate evil, and love good,
>> and establish justice in the gate.
>> —*Amos 5:14–15*

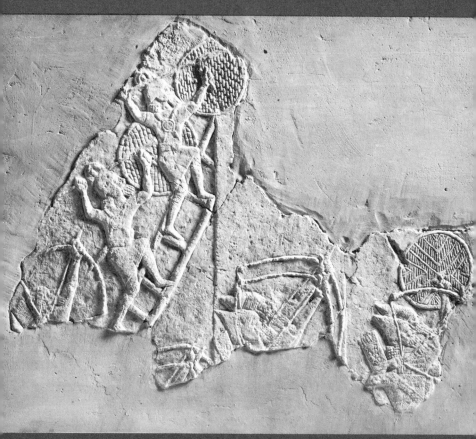

Siege of a city by the Assyrians, fragment from the palace of Sennacherib at Nineveh

THE LOVE THAT NEVER LETS GO

Israel had grown accustomed to prophets. Some of the prophets were professionals who served as members of the king's court and gave him advice. They usually saw only good things in the future, especially when their patrons were the king and his royal household. Other prophets, like Elijah and Amos, spoke for God in uncompromising terms, disdaining any connection with the professionals, the prophets and sons of prophets, as they were called. Such men cared nothing for their own safety and popularity, only for speaking the word of the LORD.

When Hosea appeared a few years after Amos had come and gone from northern Israel, he seemed different from all the other prophets. He spoke out of his own personal experience. His wife, Gomer, had borne him children and then left him to run after other men. Hosea's love for her had persisted in spite of all her infidelities. He seemed convinced that the LORD required him to take her back, even as he had commanded him to marry a harlot in the first place. So he had redeemed her, and received her again as his own.

When Hosea looked at Israel's deplorable condition, he was reminded of his marriage. Israel was like Gomer, he told the people. She had been unfaithful to God. God had taken her as his bride in the days of the wilderness, but she had been unfaithful and had run after other gods. The people had so thoroughly mixed Baal worship with Yahweh worship that they consulted Asherah (à-shē'-rá) and other fertility images for divine omens, worshiped idols, and offered sacrifices to Yahweh on hill tops where the Baal worshipers came for their rites.

Israel had flirted with other nations, too. Israel saw Assyria growing stronger in the east and tried to find protection from her might. Instead of trusting in God and his covenant as the source of strength, she made alliances with other nations, but these alliances were to be as fleeting and unstable as the morning mist.

Israel had a spirit of unfaithfulness in her, said Hosea. She did not know the LORD: she did not respond to him with her whole heart and serve him as she had promised in the days in the wilderness. Israel's love was "like a morning cloud, like the dew that goes early away."

This was not what God wanted. Said the LORD, through Hosea:

> I desire steadfast love and not sacrifice,
>   the knowledge of God, rather than burnt offerings.
>   —*Hosea 6:6*

So faithless had Israel become that there was only one way to bring her to her senses. She must be punished.

> When Israel was a child, I loved him,
>   and out of Egypt I called my son.
> The more I called them,
>   the more they went from me;
> they kept sacrificing to the Baals,
>   and burning incense to idols.
>
> Yet it was I who taught Ephraim to walk,
>   I took them up in my arms;
>   but they did not know that I healed them.
> I led them with cords of compassion,
>   with the bands of love,
> and I became to them as one
>   who eases the yoke on their jaws,
>   and I bent down to them and fed them.

> They shall return to the land of Egypt,
>> and Assyria shall be their king,
>> because they have refused to return to me.
> The sword shall rage against their cities,
>> consume the bars of their gates,
>> and devour them in their fortresses.
> My people are bent on turning away from me;
>> so they are appointed to the yoke,
>> and none shall remove it.
>
> —*Hosea 11:1–7*

But punishment was not to be meted out in blind anger. Hosea saw that God's wrath and judgment were simply expressions of a love so pure and holy that it would not let Israel go. It would cleanse Israel and restore her to her original covenant relationship of obedience to God. Her life would be renewed through the constancy of God's steadfast love.

> How can I give you up, O Ephraim!
>> How can I hand you over, O Israel! . . .
> My heart recoils within me,
>> my compassion grows warm and tender.
> I will not execute my fierce anger,
>> I will not again destroy Ephraim;
> for I am God and not man,
>> the Holy One in your midst,
>> and I will not come to destroy.
>
> —*Hosea 11:8–9*

If Israel was so unfaithful and weak that she could not return to God, then he would destroy the political alliances and the nature gods she trusted. Assyria would be his instrument of action. Released from the desire to depend on other nations, Israel would be free to be the people of the covenant and serve God. His love would not let his people go, no matter how unfaithful they had been.

This message came to Israel toward the end of the Northern Kingdom's existence. Jeroboam II was dead. One after another his successors had fought over the throne, had murdered to secure it, and had done well to live out a reign of a few years. The life of the people reflected this unstable condition. Murder, violence, and economic uncertainty ran like destructive undercurrents beneath the surface of prosperity. In the east the Assyrian shadow which had been so small in Amos' day had grown larger. Hosea saw that the armies of Assyria would overrun unstable Israel as they had the other little countries around her.

In the rise of Assyria, Hosea also saw God at work. He would use this event just as he had used events in the past. Through it he would bring Israel back to depending on her covenant relationship with him. He would make her know that he alone was her God and the source of her life; he would help her to be faithful to him again. His love was steadfast and unceasing.

Hosea was the first prophet to interpret God's love through the mirror of his own experience. He delivered his prophetic messages only a few years before the capital of the Northern Kingdom, Samaria, was captured by Assyria. When thousands of Israelites were carried away as captives to live in other provinces of the Assyrian Empire, the kingdom of Israel disappeared from the political scene.

IN QUIETNESS AND TRUST

Siloam water tunnel built by Hezekiah to supply
Jerusalem with water

Based on Isaiah 7:1–17 and 8:1–4

Judah had just as much trouble being faithful to the covenant as Israel,
her sister kingdom to the north, even
though her life as a nation was more
stable. David's descendants ruled
throughout the kingdom's history, and
her isolation from trade routes and
neighboring nations made her life less
subject to international tensions. But
Baal worship was just as great a temptation in the South as in the North.
When Assyria became the conquering
empire of the day, Judah sought alliances with other nations just as frantically as had Israel.

About ten years before the Northern Kingdom fell, a national crisis arose in the South. Judah's King Ahaz (ā' hăz) was not a very courageous ruler. A few years after he came to the throne he found that the king of Syria and the king of Israel had formed an alliance against him. They wanted to depose him, conquer Judah, and put a puppet ruler on the throne. This was a terrible prospect. The king's heart and the heart of his people "shook as the trees of the forest shake before the wind."

The only hope Ahaz could see was an alliance with Assyria. He would have to pay a huge tribute to that powerful nation, and Judah would lose her independence and become a satellite nation. But that prospect seemed less terrifying to Ahaz than being conquered by the Syrian-Israelite alliance and put off his throne. It did not seem to trouble him that signing a defense alliance also meant acknowledging Assyria's lordship in matters of religion. He would have to build an altar to Assyria's gods in the center of Jerusalem's sacred temple, alongside the altar to Yahweh.

His unfaithfulness to God did not upset Ahaz. Only the question of whether or not to call in Assyria filled his mind one day as he went out to check the city's water supply. As he reached the end of the conduit of the water system's upper pool, Ahaz unexpectedly encountered a person he knew very well: Isaiah, the prophet of the LORD. The prophet seemed to know what the unhappy king was thinking.

"Don't be alarmed by the threats of the king of Syria and the king of Israel," he said to Ahaz. "They are no more dangerous than smoldering stumps of wood. They're not real firebrands. Their alliance won't amount to anything. It will be broken soon by Assyria, and the danger to Judah will be overcome by the LORD himself acting through Assyria. Do not be afraid. And above all, do not call on Assyria for help. That would be foolish. Only trust in God and wait patiently."

Ahaz looked at Isaiah in amazement. What he had just said sounded like nonsense to Ahaz. With two invaders camped on his doorstep, how could such advice be worth the time it took to utter it? Trust in the LORD? Ahaz had not the least idea what Isaiah meant. He laughed at the prophet and went about his business.

Isaiah did not give up his attempts to persuade Ahaz not to call on Assyria for help. He had studied the international scene and believed that Assyria would soon overthrow this feeble Syrian-Israelite alliance. What was more, he was sure that this was the work of God, the holy God of Israel who summoned all nations to work out his purposes, whether they knew it or not. Faith in this holy God, the true king of the whole world, was the only practical basis for living, believed Isaiah. It was better to wait patiently for God's way to be known than to clutch frantically at this straw or that whenever a crisis arose. In quietness and confidence lay the only security.

On another occasion the prophet tried to get Ahaz to believe that Yahweh had doomed the Syrian-Israelite alliance. He told the king to ask God for a sign to confirm the warning Isaiah had already issued in the LORD's name.

"A sign?" asked Ahaz skeptically. He knew that to religious people like Isaiah a sign would be some everyday activity that would remind him of God's participation in his affairs. But the king wanted none of such foolishness, especially when he had such a difficult problem on his hands.

He shook his head impatiently, then added piously, "I do not wish to put the LORD to the test."

Isaiah responded quickly. "Very well, O king. If you will not trust God enough to ask for a sign, he will give you one himself. He will put *you* to the test. A child will be born to a young woman, and he will be named Immanuel, God is with us. Before he is old enough to tell the evil from the good, that is, while he is still very young, the land before whose two kings you tremble will be deserted. The Syrian-Israelite alliance will have been broken up. But this will not save you now. It is too late for you and your lack of trust in God. The LORD will bring upon you and your people terrible hardship and trouble worse than you have ever known. The king of Assyria will sweep through your land!"

Isaiah was saying that Assyria would actually invade Judah if Ahaz made an alliance with her. But even this did not shake Ahaz in his determination to call for help. He could not and would not trust God.

41

Isaiah tried a third time to convince the king that the alliance would fail and Judah would be saved without Assyrian help. When Isaiah's second son was born, he gave him a symbolic name that meant, "The spoil speeds, the prey hastes." Isaiah testified that the wealth of Damascus and the splendor of Samaria would be carried away by the king of Assyria before the child could say the words "My father."

Ahaz was as deaf as ever to the word of the LORD that Isaiah brought him. He had made up his mind. Messengers were sent to the king of Assyria with this plea: "I am your servant and your son. Come up, and rescue me from the hand of the king of Syria and from the hand of the king of Israel, who are attacking me." Along with this SOS Ahaz sent silver and gold vessels from Yahweh's temple and whatever treasures he could spare from his own palace.

The king of Assyria, who bore the formidable name of Tiglath-pileser (tĭg' lăth-pĭ-lē' zĕr), was only too glad to respond to Ahaz' plea. What monarch bent on conquering the world would not have been pleased to receive an invitation to take over part of it without having to fight for it? He swept down upon Damascus, conquered the city, sent its people away captives, and killed its king.

Ahaz went to Damascus to meet the lord before whom he now had to bow. He saw the altar to the Assyrian gods there, had it copied, and placed it in the center of the temple of the holy God of Israel in whom he had refused to trust. Ahaz had gained temporary safety from attack by surrendering Judah's freedom to the nation which was determined to rule all other nations.

In Jerusalem Isaiah went about his life in the quietness and confidence of which he had spoken to Ahaz. He would wait patiently until God again called him to speak to Judah in his name. He, his disciples, and his children would be living signs of God's presence among the people. For thus said the LORD, the Holy One of Israel,

> "In returning and rest you shall be saved;
> in quietness and in trust shall be your strength."
> —*Isaiah 30:15*

In Isaiah of Jerusalem those who were not blind saw what it meant to trust the God of the covenant.

OUTSIDE OR INSIDE?

Based on 2 Kings 22; 23:1–30

For the next century Assyria ruled the world, and Judah had her ups and downs. Good King Hezekiah (hĕz-ĕ-kī′ å) followed unbelieving Ahaz on the Southern Kingdom's throne. Hezekiah loved God sincerely and introduced sweeping reforms in Judah's worship. All the local shrines or high places where pillars, Asherah poles, and Baal images had been worshiped were destroyed. Ahaz' detested shrine to the Assyrian gods was removed from the temple, and all Judah was urged to worship there.

In another national crisis when Assyrian armies camped outside the walls of Jerusalem and ordered the city to surrender, Isaiah, the prophet, once more advised the king to trust God. This time the king listened to the prophet. Despite taunts and threats to Hezekiah by the Assyrian general, his army retreated one night, and Jerusalem was saved.

The best king of Judah was succeeded by the worst. Manasseh (mà-nă′ sĕ) was as faithless to God as his father Hezekiah had been devoted. For fifty years he degraded and corrupted worship of the Holy One of Israel. All that the prophets had spoken against for centuries was honored in the reign of the renegade Manasseh. To make matters even worse, Assyrian magic and astrology were added to the temple worship, and human sacrifice was practiced.

During these years Assyria reached the very zenith of her glory. Her proud armies tramped up and down the land surrounding little Judah, but because Manasseh was a faithful, obedient vassal of the empire, his land was left alone. The people came to believe that as long as a descendant of David was on the throne, God had to look favorably on Judah. No matter how sinful the nation might be, how many other gods she might worship, or how much injustice and corruption might flourish in the land, if David's line still ruled, God had to defend David and David's city, Jerusalem. The belief developed that God had made a special covenant with David, which he would not break.

The prophets of the Northern Kingdom would never have recognized this as the covenant. Nor would prophets who were yet to arise in the Southern Kingdom. But during this dark period in Judah's history, no prophets spoke. The word of the LORD seemed to have been silenced.

Then came another king, a good king—Josiah (jō-sī′ à). Grandson of Manasseh, he inherited the good qualities of his great-grandfather, Hezekiah. "He did what was right in the eyes of the LORD," wrote a historian.

When young Josiah came to the throne, the end of Assyria's power could be foreseen. Suppressed peoples were trying to throw off her iron rule. Nations were asserting their independence. Local customs and religions were being revived. Judah fell in line. Because he was a faithful worshiper of God, Josiah decided to repair the temple and clear out all traces of Assyrian and Baal worship. One day he sent his secretary, Shaphan (shā′ făn), to the temple to settle accounts for the expenses of restoration with Hilkiah (hĭl-kī′ ă), the high priest.

Hilkiah gave Shaphan a startling bit of news. "We have found a book in the temple," he announced. "It is the book of the law."

For many years the law, or the commandments of the covenant, had not been read to the people. The annual covenant renewal ceremony had not been held since anyone could remember, nor could people remember hearing their fathers or their grandfathers speak of it. Shaphan hurried back to the king and made his financial report. Then he produced the scroll that Hilkiah had found. "Hilkiah the priest has given me a book," he remarked. "I think I should read it to you."

What Shaphan read had an astounding effect upon Josiah. The king tore his robe—a sign of great despair—and spoke in anguished tones. "Our fathers have not done what the words of this book command!" he exclaimed. "The wrath of the LORD will be aroused against us, and we will suffer for their sins. Woe is me, that we should suffer for such disobedience. Go and consult a prophet of the LORD to see what we must do."

The king's secretaries and the high priest hurried to the home of Huldah (hūl′dȧ), a prophetess who lived in Jerusalem. She assured them that evil would come upon the inhabitants of Judah because they had done what the words of the book prohibited. They had worshiped false gods. But because the king had been penitent, the LORD would spare him the sight of the punishment that would come upon the land.

King Josiah lost no time in calling all the people of Judah and Jerusalem together at the temple. In their hearing the king read the book of the covenant which had been found in the temple, just as Moses and Joshua had read the law to the companies assembled at the mountain and at Shechem. They renewed the covenant to walk in the ways of the LORD, to keep his commandments with all their heart and soul, and to perform the words of the covenant as they were written in the book.

A great reform followed. Every idolatrous practice was wiped out. Worship was centralized in the temple; high places and local shrines were demolished. Altars in every place but the temple were destroyed. Priests were allowed to officiate only in Jerusalem. Every injunction in the book of the covenant was followed to the letter. Josiah even ordered that the Passover be celebrated once again.

Year after year Josiah diligently saw to it that the reforms in worship and conduct were maintained. There never had been anything like this effort before. What was the book that started this amazing change? Probably the central portion of the book of Deuteronomy.

Written as though it were a farewell sermon by Moses, the book contained many injunctions about how worship was to be conducted, what feasts were to be observed, and how the people were to treat one another and live in the land promised to them. As long as they obeyed these commandments, they would prosper and receive God's blessing. If they disobeyed, evil and hard times would come upon them. "Therefore you shall keep his statutes and his commandments, which I command you this day, that it may go well with you, and with your children after you, and that you may prolong your days in the land which the LORD your God gives you for ever," read the book. (Deuteronomy 4:40)

All Judah followed her king in trying to apply this book-directed religion. The fear of punishment hung over the people, for the book stated that the wrath of the LORD would be visited upon them if they failed to keep the covenant. And the book promised the reward of God's blessing if they kept the laws.

Then came news that seemed too terrible to be true. Good King Josiah was dead, killed in battle at the age of forty! The nation was stunned. After the first shock people began to ask questions. If obedience to the covenant in the book was rewarded with long life and God's blessing, why had this good king died so young? He above all others had been zealous in obeying the commandments of the book.

Without the example of their leader, the reform faded. Worship became less pure. People were less concerned to keep all the requirements of the law. The compulsion to obey had been destroyed, for goodness in the king had not been rewarded with long life.

Josiah's reform had not touched enough upon the inner fundamentals of keeping the covenant that the great prophets had proclaimed: justice, steadfast love, wholehearted response to God, quiet trust, and patient waiting. The good king's reform had touched chiefly the external practices. These were easily forgotten when the inner attitudes of the heart were not changed, and when the incentive to behave differently on the outside was removed.

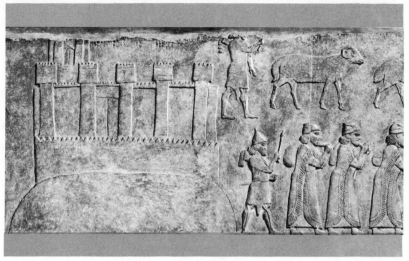

Captives being deported from the city of Ashtaroth, eighth century. Bas-relief of Tiglath-pileser

UPON THEIR HEARTS

At the height of Josiah's reform, when things seemed to be going well for Judah, no one knew better than the prophet Jeremiah that the end for the nation was not far off. All his life he had longed for a peaceful, retiring existence in his native village of Anathoth. But God had decreed otherwise. He had called Jeremiah when he was less than twenty years old and had made him his prophet:

"Before I formed you in the womb I knew you,
and before you were born I consecrated you;
I appointed you a prophet to the nations. . . .
Do not say, 'I am only a youth';
for to all to whom I send you you shall go,
and whatever I command you you shall speak.
Be not afraid of them,
for I am with you to deliver you,
    says the LORD. . . .
Behold, I have put my words in your mouth.
See, I have set you this day over nations and over kingdoms,
to pluck up and to break down,
to destroy and to overthrow,
to build and to plant."

—Jeremiah 1:5–10

47

Never had Jeremiah been able to set aside that call. For the rest of his life he told the people of Jerusalem how they had sinned against God. They had turned their backs on the God who had saved them and made them a people; they had even tried to make their own gods—which proved about as effective as unplastered and leaky cisterns. Again and again Judah, like Israel, had been faithless to her God; and again and again, through the events of her life, Yahweh had tried to persuade his faithless people to return to him.

Jeremiah suffered deeply as he proclaimed his message from the LORD. The wounds of his people wounded him. He felt the tragedy of their sins and agonized over the faithlessness of their covenant-breaking:

> My grief is beyond healing,
>> my heart is sick within me. . . .
> For the wound of the daughter of my people
>> is my heart wounded,
>> I mourn, and dismay has taken hold on me.
>
> Is there no balm in Gilead?
>> Is there no physician there?
>> —*Jeremiah 8:18–22*

All the suffering that the people of Judah had brought on themselves seemed to flow through Jeremiah's heart. Yet God had called him to warn the people that an enemy from the north would be the instrument of Yahweh's judgment, and warn them he did.

Year in and year out he spoke for the LORD. The high priest became so angry at his words that he forbade Jeremiah to enter the temple again. The prophet was put in stocks. He was shunned by the people, denounced as a traitor. When he had his faithful secretary write out his message on a scroll and send it to the king, the monarch cut it into shreds and contemptuously burned it.

When Assyria fell, Babylonia took her place as the reigning power of the world. Jeremiah saw Judah's doom in the advance of the armies of Nebuchadnezzar (něb' ŭ-kåd-něz' ěr), king of Babylonia. Jeremiah believed that Judah would be conquered and many of her people exiled. But in that doom as a nation Jeremiah also saw hope.

He advised the royal court to surrender peacefully to Babylon. God would use the time of exile to cleanse Judah and transform her so that the ancient promise to Abraham might come true: all nations might bless themselves through her.

At this message, the king's courtiers denounced Jeremiah as a traitor and threw him into a slimy cistern. The armies of Babylonia came, besieged the city, and carried the cream of Judah's leadership off to exile. Jeremiah remained in Jerusalem where the word of the LORD came to him in a vision. He saw two baskets of figs. One was full of good ripe figs; the other contained rotten ones. The exiles were the good figs. They would return to God with their whole hearts, and when the time of their punishment was over, God would bring them back to their land. But the puppet king and his courtiers who remained in Judah were the bad figs. They would be utterly destroyed.

Jeremiah saw that the people's only hope was in exile. Naturally no one believed him. Then he wrote a letter to the exiles in Babylon urging them to settle down for a long stay. They were to be faithful to God, even though there was no temple for their worship in that strange land. God was where his people were; he was not limited to one country, as they had always thought. Jeremiah wrote,

"Thus says the LORD: When seventy years are completed for Babylon, I will visit you, and I will fulfil to you my promise and bring you back to this place. For I know the plans I have for you, says the LORD, plans for welfare and not for evil, to give you a future and a hope. . . . You will seek me and find me; when you seek me with all your heart, I will be found by you, says the LORD, and I will restore your fortunes and gather you from all the nations . . . and I will bring you back to the place from which I sent you into exile."
—*Jeremiah 29:10–14*

For holding out such comforting words of hope and assurance, all Jeremiah received was a complaint to headquarters by an official of the exiles in Babylon. Why hadn't the authorities in Jerusalem rebuked this prophet for discouraging the exiles by predicting that they would have to stay in Babylon a long time?

To the end of his days Jeremiah pleaded with Judah to accept her punishment as the way of restoration to covenant relationship

with the LORD. A wicked, deceitful heart was the cause of her unfaithfulness. But in the fullness of time God would give a new
covenant. It would be an inner covenant of the heart, not the old,
external one of obedience to law.

> Thus says the LORD: . . .
> "I have loved you with an everlasting love;
>> therefore I have continued my faithfulness to you.
> Again I will build you, and you shall be built, . . .
> There is hope for your future,
>> says the LORD,
> and your children shall come back to their own country. . . .

"And it shall come to pass that as I have watched over them to pluck
up and break down, to overthrow, destroy, and bring evil, so I will
watch over them to build and to plant, . . .

"Behold, the days are coming, says the LORD, when I will make a
new covenant with the house of Israel and the house of Judah, not
like the covenant which I made with their fathers when I took them
by the hand to bring them out of the land of Egypt, my covenant
which they broke, . . . But this is the covenant which I will make
. . . says the LORD: I will put my law within them, and I will write
it upon their hearts; and I will be their God, and they shall be my
people . . . . for I will forgive their iniquity, and I will remember
their sin no more."

—Jeremiah 31:2–4, 17, 28–34

The nation that had come to birth as the covenant people of God
was dead. It had broken the covenant. It had lost the Promised
Land. Yet Jeremiah saw great hope for the faithless people: God
would again make a covenant, a new covenant which would be forever written on the hearts of the people. They would know God and
be faithful to him, and he would be their God.

Painting of a reconstruction of the Ishtar Gate, Babylon

IN THE MIDST OF THEM

Vision of dry bones based on Ezekiel 37:1–14

After nearly a dozen years in the land of Babylonia, the exiles began to find life not too unbearable. In their little colonies on the canal outside the magnificent capital city of Babylon itself, they could carry on their own way of life. Processions, festivals, the pomp of armies, and Babylon's glorious culture made life colorful and fascinating. Memories of little Jerusalem and the modest temple of God, which had once seemed so marvelous, began to fade a little. Marduk (mär′ dūk), god of Babylon, seemed to be a mighty god too. Had he not sponsored this nation of opulence and splendor?

But the splendor of Babylon could not blot out completely the memory of the city of Zion and the temple of its God. The exiles continued to long for home. Jerusalem was still standing. Could it be true, as Jeremiah had written, that they might one day see its beloved walls again and go to the temple to offer to Yahweh the sacrifices that were more than life itself to the devout Jew?

Toward the end of the twelfth year of exile their hope was dashed. Jerusalem was destroyed. Wails of anguish broke out when the news was received. The colony of exiles went into deepest mourning. King Nebuchadnezzar's Babylonian armies had sacked the city. Its walls had been broken down. The temple had been burned. The line of David no longer sat upon the throne. Judah had gone the way of Israel. Fallen was the nation; the people of God were without their land.

Bitterness and despair filled the hearts of the exiles. Where was their God now?

An answer came, strangely enough, from one of their own group in Babylonia who had been deported with them a dozen years earlier. A priest had become a prophet of the LORD early in the exile. In vision after vision this man, Ezekiel, had seen doom coming upon Judah because the people had betrayed their God and rejected their obligations to him. The LORD's glory and overwhelming holiness had been stained by his people's impure actions. Such impurity and falseness could not stand in God's presence. The nation had to be punished and God's name and majesty upheld before the nations. Such was the word of the LORD which the prophet Ezekiel spoke during the early days of exile.

But after Jerusalem fell, Ezekiel's message changed. The doom he had foretold had come to pass. Now he had a word of hope. The house of Israel would be restored. It had been destroyed, but God would make it new so that his way might be known. Again and again Ezekiel announced this astonishing news:

"Thus says the Lord GOD: It is not for your sake, O house of Israel, that I am about to act, but for the sake of my holy name, which you have profaned among the nations to which you came. . . . For I will take you from the nations, and gather you from all the countries, and bring you into your own land. I will sprinkle clean water upon

Painting of a reconstruction of Babylon in Nebuchadnezzar's time

you, and you shall be clean from all your uncleannesses, and from all your idols I will cleanse you. A new heart I will give you, and a new spirit I will put within you; and I will take out of your flesh the heart of stone and give you a heart of flesh. And I will put my spirit within you, and cause you to walk in my statutes and be careful to observe my ordinances."

—*Ezekiel 36:22–27*

There was no mistaking what Ezekiel said. God was about to perform a mighty act. He would save the people so that all nations might know his holiness and purity. The vision of the valley of dry bones made this message even plainer.

The Spirit of the LORD, said Ezekiel, had taken him into a valley filled with old, dry bones. The LORD had commanded Ezekiel to say to these bones, "Hear the word of the LORD: I will cause breath to enter you, and you shall live." They would then be clothed in sinews, flesh, and skin, and breath would be put in them!

Ezekiel had done as the LORD commanded. He had heard a rattling. The bones came together, bone to its bone. Sinews joined them; flesh covered them; skin encased them. The LORD ordered Ezekiel to call the four winds to put breath into these reconnected bones. Ezekiel had obeyed, and the bones lived.

The bones, said Ezekiel, were the whole house of Israel—south and north, Judah and Israel. They had been saying just what the exiles had said: "Our hope is lost; we are clean cut off." But behold, the LORD would open their graves, raise them up, and bring them home to the land of Israel.

Ezekiel ended the report of his vision with the word of hope that was his new message: "Thus says the LORD, 'And you shall know that I am the LORD, when I open your graves, and raise you from your graves, O my people. And I will put my Spirit within you, and you shall live, . . . then you shall know that I, the LORD, have spoken, and I have done it.'"

No exile could think for a moment that he deserved this new life. God would give it so that the people might know that he was the LORD. Furthermore, said Ezekiel, the LORD would make an everlasting covenant of peace with them. He would put his sanctuary in their midst. The temple, restored and more glorious than ever before, would stand at the center of their life. The whole nation would be like a church with the priests ruling it in the name of God.

"My dwelling place shall be with them; and I will be their God, and they shall be my people," was Ezekiel's word from the LORD. (Ezekiel 37:27)

Ezekiel's vision of the future was so graphic that he even laid out all the details of the temple and what would happen in it. The people would no longer defile God's name by their idolatry and faithlessness. Other nations would know that the LORD blessed Israel, for his dwelling place would be the heart of the nation's life forevermore.

Years later, when the exiles went home, they remembered vividly what Ezekiel had said.

Ivory cherub from Samaria. Ezekiel's vision included cherubim

THE GLORY OF THE LORD

Ezekiel's vision of a restored temple and renewed holiness became reality, but not right away. Jeremiah had seen what the people needed when he told them that they would be in exile for a long time. The early Hebrews had to wander in the wilderness long enough to find out what it meant to live by obligations to God and in mutual concern for one another. Now the exiles had to have time to discover all over again who Yahweh was and what he, their God, expected of them. For centuries the people of Israel had mixed other kinds of worship and other ideas of the divine with the beliefs they brought from the exodus to the Promised Land. The whole people had lost true knowledge of God. Their ideas and their way of living had to be cleansed. Both Jeremiah and Ezekiel were right. The people had to have a new inner spirit.

Painful though they were, the years after Jerusalem's fall were this time of cleansing for the exiles. The people gathered in homes to study the story of their past. They thought about the mighty deeds of their God on their behalf. They read and reread the traditions of Moses. The words of the great prophets burned in their consciousness as they looked back on those unheeded warnings to keep God's covenant or perish as a nation. Isaiah of Jerusalem had been right in saying that Assyria was a rod of punishment in the hand of God. Jeremiah had seen correctly that Nebuchadnezzar was an instrument of God's purpose.

The false worship from the days of Baalism disappeared. Pagan practices from Assyrian cults vanished. Even the temptations offered by Marduk's glory were resisted. It began to come clearer to this remnant of the tribe of Judah, now called the Jews, who Yahweh was and what his covenant with his people meant.

About half a century after Jerusalem fell, the greatest of the long line of Hebrew spokesmen for God put the smoldering hopes of the people into words. His messages rang with triumph, joy, and exultation. Their glory reflected the glory of the just and merciful God whose power and love the prophet proclaimed. He lived among the exiles in Babylon and today is referred to as Second Isaiah, or Isaiah of the Exile.

God was about to act again, he said. The exodus from Egypt had been a mighty deed wrought by the strong hand of God, but now a new exodus would be greater still.

> Comfort, comfort my people,
>   says your God.
> Speak tenderly to Jerusalem,
>   and cry to her
> that her warfare is ended,
>   that her iniquity is pardoned,
> that she has received from the LORD's hand
>   double for all her sins.

A voice cries:
"In the wilderness prepare the way of the LORD,
    make straight in the desert a highway for our God.
Every valley shall be lifted up,
    and every mountain and hill be made low;
the uneven ground shall become level,
    and the rough places a plain.
And the glory of the LORD shall be revealed,
    and all flesh shall see it together."

—Isaiah 40:1–5

How would this great exodus be accomplished? By the hand of one who did not know Yahweh as his God. By the hand of Cyrus, king of Persia, whom God had anointed to be his agent. The second Isaiah, prophet of the exile, saw the kingdom of Persia rising in power. He saw that Babylonia would go down before it. Already countries to the north and east had fallen. The Persian leader, Cyrus, was a merciful monarch. He let some of the conquered kings remain on their thrones. He restored places of worship and returned gold and silver which Babylonia or Assyria had carried off. Isaiah of the Exile saw that Yahweh would use Cyrus, one of the most enlightened rulers history had seen, to authorize the return of the Jews and the rebuilding of the temple.

Thus says the LORD to his anointed, to Cyrus,
    whose right hand I have grasped,
to subdue nations before him
    and ungird the loins of kings, . . .
"I will go before you
    and level the mountains, . . .
that you may know that it is I, the LORD,
    the God of Israel, who call you by your name.
For the sake of my servant Jacob,
    and Israel my chosen,
I call you by your name,
    I surname you, though you do not know me.
I am the LORD, and there is no other,
    besides me there is no God."

—Isaiah 45:1–5

At last the great news had dawned upon Israel: There was no other God in all the earth—only Yahweh, the Lord of hosts, the Redeemer of Israel, existed. He ruled all nations. He had created the earth. All things were under his control.

> The LORD is the everlasting God,
> > the Creator of the ends of the earth.
> He does not faint or grow weary,
> > his understanding is unsearchable.
> He gives power to the faint,
> > and to him who has no might he increases strength.
> Even youths shall faint and be weary,
> > and young men shall fall exhausted;
> but they who wait for the LORD shall renew their strength,
> > they shall mount up with wings like eagles,
> they shall run and not be weary,
> > they shall walk and not faint.
>
> *—Isaiah 40:28b–31*

If people would trust in God, then they would know him and receive strength to bear their tribulations. They would rejoice and go out with singing. Their new life would be filled with joy and peace that nothing could take away. The LORD's purpose would be fulfilled. He would be made known to all peoples, even to the end of the earth. Israel's mission was to make him known. Through the life of the nation, and the people who made up that nation, God's love and justice were to be proclaimed. As the people of the covenant, both living in the Promised Land and in exile and sorrow, they were meant to be God's servants. The servant of the LORD was a suffering servant, but through his faithfulness to God's will he would tell all nations of this God who is the only God in all the earth. Little Israel, trampled upon and least of nations, was to tell the earth's kings of the LORD, righteous God and Savior. This task, laid upon Israel, would make her hardships and tribulations a cause for rejoicing.

> So shall he startle many nations;
> > kings shall shut their mouths because of him;

Scroll of the book of Isaiah dating from c. 100 B.C. found at Khirbet Qumran, 1947

for that which has not been told them they shall see,
    and that which they have not heard they shall under-
       stand. . . .
He was despised and rejected by men;
    a man of sorrows, and acquainted with grief;
and as one from whom men hide their faces
    he was despised, and we esteemed him not.

Surely he has borne our griefs
    and carried our sorrows;
yet we esteemed him stricken,
    smitten by God, and afflicted.
But he was wounded for our transgressions,
    he was bruised for our iniquities;
upon him was the chastisement that made us whole,
    and with his stripes we are healed.
                        —Isaiah 52:15; 53:3–5

In the purpose of God, which is too great for man to understand, Israel was to be the servant of the Lord, the agent of Yahweh. How great would be the servant's joy to see that through his suffering other nations would be brought to worship God and know his love! Sorrow and destruction would be worth while when such results were produced, and the servant would rejoice that he had been called to this task.

So Isaiah of the Exile saw the meaning of all that had happened to Israel. It was for a purpose far beyond man's understanding, but one that he could see now as he looked back upon the past and forward with hope to the future.

> Behold, you shall call nations that you know not,
>   and nations that knew you not shall run to you,
> because of the Lord your God, and of the Holy One of Israel,
>   for he has glorified you.
>
> Seek the Lord while he may be found,
>   call upon him while he is near;
> let the wicked forsake his way,
>   and the unrighteous man his thoughts;
> let him return to the Lord, that he may have mercy on him,
>   and to our God, for he will abundantly pardon.
> For my thoughts are not your thoughts,
>   neither are your ways my ways, says the Lord.
> For as the heavens are higher than the earth,
>   so are my ways higher than your ways
>   and my thoughts than your thoughts.
>
> For as the rain and the snow come down from heaven,
>   and return not thither but water the earth,
> making it bring forth and sprout,
>   giving seed to the sower and bread to the eater,
> so shall my word be that goes forth from my mouth;
>   it shall not return to me empty,
> but it shall accomplish that which I purpose,
>   and prosper in the thing for which I sent it.
> —*Isaiah 55:5–11*

Isaiah of the Exile had learned what the new spirit within Israel had to be.

HOME AGAIN

Based on Ezra 1; 3–7 and Nehemiah 8–9

Like the other prophets, Isaiah of the Exile had read correctly what was happening in history. The first year after Cyrus of Persia conquered Babylon, he issued this edict:

> "Thus says Cyrus king of Persia: The LORD, the God of heaven, has given me all the kingdoms of the earth, and he has charged me to build him a house at Jerusalem, which is in Judah. Whoever is among you of all his people, may his God be with him, and let him go up to Jerusalem, which is in Judah, and rebuild the house of the LORD, the God of Israel—he is the God who is in Jerusalem; and let each survivor, in whatever place he sojourns, be assisted by the men of his place with silver and gold, with goods and with beasts, besides freewill offerings for the house of God which is in Jerusalem."
>
> —*Ezra 1:2–4*

And so the exile ended. But not all the Jews wanted to go back to Jerusalem, now that they were free. Life in Babylonia had grown comfortable; business was flourishing. Many of them preferred to stay where they were. But several thousand did return, armed with Cyrus' edict and the treasures of the temple that Nebuchadnezzar had stolen as loot long years before.

The Jerusalem they found was a pitiful sight. The city's walls were broken down, the temple a pile of rubble. Fields around the city had grown up to weeds. Here and there farmers were trying to raise crops, but the soil was thin and eroded. Vineyards had grown up to briers. Houses had tumbled down. Neighbors to the north (Samaria) and south (Edom) were anything but glad to see the exiles return. They resented their presence.

The exiles discovered that they had returned to a backwoods, run-down, poverty-stricken, little province of a great empire. Isaiah of the Exile's glorious picture of the joy of returning and the fruits of the servant's sacrificial labors seemed far away, a golden dream that had faded.

Reconstruction began painfully. An altar on the ruins of the old temple was the best the exiles could do at first. When a new governor—a descendant of David—came several years later, things looked brighter. Foundations for the new temple were laid. It was a great day for the people. Dressed in their most elaborate robes the priests and the music directors formed a procession. Trumpets sounded, cymbals clashed, and the choirs sang the responsive chant so familiar in the worship in the old temple:

> "For he is good,
>   for his steadfast love endures for ever toward Israel."
>
> —*Ezra 3:11b*

Men shouted and wept for joy.

It took five years to finish the temple. Most of that time the tools of the workmen lay idle because the Samaritans, whose offer to help with the temple had been spurned, now tried to prevent the rebuilding altogether. Samaritans were not of pure Jewish blood since they had intermarried with Assyrian prisoners of war after the Northern Kingdom fell. The returning exiles feared that unless they kept strictly to themselves their religion would soon be corrupted by false practices. They were determined that Israel would not fail her God this time.

Finally the temple was completed. Compared to Solomon's temple it was small and unimpressive. But it was more beautiful than all Babylon in the eyes of the faithful. The devout worshiper longed to spend all his days in the house of the LORD. As he heard the Levites chant the psalms of praise, or presented his offerings and watched the smoke curl upward from the altar, he felt comforted, forgiven, filled with hope.

Enemies might press hard upon the people from every side, life might be grim and a struggle, but in the temple worship, the Jewish people felt at one with their God, and life seemed good.

At the times of the great festivals—the Passover, Pentecost, Tabernacles—pilgrims came from every quarter to the Holy City, Zion, to give thanks to God in the temple. Choirs sang the psalms which expressed the faith of the people. They poured out their praise to God, implored his pardon for their sins, and besought his aid in times of crisis.

> Praise the LORD!
> Praise the LORD, O my soul!
> I will praise the LORD as long as I live;
>   I will sing praises to my God while I have being.
>
> Put not your trust in princes,
>   in a son of man, in whom there is no help.
> When his breath departs he returns to his earth;
>   on the very day his plans perish.
>
> Happy is he whose help is the God of Jacob,
>   whose hope is in the LORD his God.
>   —*Psalm 146:1–5*

The exiles returned by several stages, over a period of many years. Nehemiah came first and helped rebuild the walls of Jerusalem. Ezra, the scribe, came later with a special commission from Artaxerxes (är-tăk-sûrk′ sēz), then the king of Persia. Ezra was commissioned to study the religious situation, particularly the law, and to teach the people of Jerusalem its statutes and ordinances again so they might have a pattern for their daily life. Many exiles returned to Jerusalem with Ezra.

When Ezra reached Jerusalem, the people gathered gladly to hear him. He stood on a wooden pulpit raised above the heads of the crowd. In his hands he held the book of the law, written on a scroll. The people waited expectantly. He opened the scroll. In their generation, and in the generations of their fathers, no one had read the law to them.

"Praise ye the LORD!" chanted Ezra.

"Amen! Amen!" the people answered, and bowed their heads to the ground and worshiped. The old, old ritual was known to them even though the words of the law were not.

Ezra began to read, and kept on reading from early morning

until the middle of the day. The scribes translated difficult passages into Aramaic—the popular language—so that the people understood what they heard. As they heard the word of the LORD, which was so fundamental to their lives, the people wept, partly with joy, partly with grief at having neglected it so long.

"This day is holy to the LORD your God!" said Ezra when the reading was finished. "Do not mourn or weep, but go on your way rejoicing, for the joy of the LORD is your strength."

The time of the feast of the booths, or Tabernacles, came. As the law commanded, the people went out and cut olive and myrtle and palm branches and made booths. The rooftops of the houses, the courtyards of homes, the courts of the house of God, and the city squares at the gates of Jerusalem were covered with booths, in remembrance of the time when the people had wandered in the wilderness.

For seven days the festival continued. Every day Ezra read further from the law. He recalled the history of the people and prayed God to remember his covenant with them. "Now therefore," he said, "our God, the great and mighty and terrible God, who keepest covenant and steadfast love, let not all the hardship seem little to thee that has come upon us. Yet thou hast been just in all that has come upon us, for thou hast dealt faithfully and we have acted wickedly. Because of all this we make a firm covenant and write it before thee." And Ezra set before the people the law as their covenant.

All the people signed the covenant. The governor and the priests and the Levites set their seal to it. Once more the people of Israel had renewed the covenant with their God. They took an oath to observe all the commandments of the LORD and all his ordinances and statutes.

Their intentions were of the best. The Jews wanted to keep from corrupting their religion by outside influences. As the years passed, they succeeded in doing this. But in the process the *letter* of the law became their master, and they obscured the *spirit* of the law which was love for God and neighbor. The new covenant, written on their hearts, and the new spirit within them, had not yet fully come to the people settled in the province of Judah.

THE LAST SUPPER, Ravenna mosaic, sixth century A.D.

GOOD NEWS OF A GREAT JOY TO ALL PEOPLE

Time and empires marched on as they had for centuries, but the little province of Judah clung to its temple-centered worship and to its daily life regulated by all the details of the law. Centuries passed, and the Persian Empire gave away to the Greek, the Greek to the Seleucid, and the Seleucid to the Roman. Whoever their ruler and whatever the time, the Jews were determined to be loyal to their sacred heritage, no matter what the cost.

Scribes and rabbis tried to keep the law's demands up-to-date to meet changing conditions. They handed down oral interpretations of the original law in the Pentateuch, telling the people what to do in order to carry out the law in every part of life. The written law with its interpretations was called the Torah. Five hundred years after the exile ended, there were so many petty rules and regulations that the poor laboring classes found it almost impossible to obey all the rules and earn a living at the same time.

By this time the Jewish people had also developed a strong hope for the future. It wasn't Jeremiah's hope for a new covenant of the heart, although of course people knew about that. Neither was the hope of the Jews focused in the portrait of the servant who would suffer gladly in order to tell other nations about God, which had been the vision of Isaiah of the Exile. The Jews now expected God to take a direct hand in bringing a more glorious future. One of two things might happen. An ideal ruler would establish God's righteousness and peace throughout the world, with an important place for the faithful Jews. Or God himself would bring in his rule by sending a messiah to announce divine victory over the evil powers in the world.

By the middle of what we call the first century after Christ, the poor in Palestine longed for release from their burdens, and the rebellious longed for a deliverer. But the nation itself was just as much under the heel of Roman rule as it ever had been. Nothing seemed to have happened. Nothing, that is, except in one small group of people. These people claimed that God already had brought in his kingdom. He already had begun his rule on earth among men!

In the person of a man named Jesus of Nazareth, these people claimed that God had fulfilled all the promises made to Israel through the law and the prophets. The new covenant had come, they said. A new people of God had been called into being. Anyone who believed that God had revealed himself in the life, the death, and the resurrection of this man Jesus might belong. God had acted, once and for all, fully and completely. This was good news of a great joy for all people!

If a Roman official heard this news, he probably shrugged his shoulders and went about his business as usual. These new religious sects were constantly springing up. What difference did one more make, so long as it didn't start an uprising?

Historians of the time paid no attention to the extraordinary claims of these people. Only one writer even mentioned the name *Jesus*, and that in a brief sentence.

The Jews themselves were divided. Some believed that Jesus was the fulfillment of the old covenant, the bringer of the new. In Jerusalem, not long after Jesus had been executed by crucifixion, the manner reserved for criminals, thousands heard Peter and other disciples of Jesus preach. They listened to the message— Jesus is risen from the dead; he is the Christ—and were converted. The new believers lived quietly, shared all they had with one another, and worshiped God daily in the temple with prayer and thanksgiving.

Other Jews had once been attracted to Jesus. When he had ridden into Jerusalem for the Passover they had thought he was the promised messiah, the ideal ruler, and they had cheered him with the royal welcome: "Hosanna! Blessed is he who comes in the name of the Lord!" But then nothing had happened. No kingdom, no overthrow of Rome, nothing. The people had lost their enthusiasm. They had not cared when it turned out that after all Jesus was a blasphemer, not a prophet. Let him die!

Some Jews, like a rabbi from Tarsus named Saul, feared the growing power of the followers of this Risen Christ. They killed their leaders, men like Stephen. They determined at all costs to wipe out this sect which declared that the law had been fulfilled in the man of Nazareth.

The temple authorities also opposed the followers of Jesus. At one time Peter and John were arrested for preaching and healing in the name and power of Jesus the Christ. The temple authorities warned them not to preach and heal again or they would be killed. Peter had looked them in the eye. "Whether it is right in the sight of God to listen to you rather than to God, you must judge; for we cannot but speak of what we have seen and heard," he had replied boldly. (Acts 4:19–20) The authorities had let them go because the people supported Peter and John.

The believers gradually grew into the Christian church. Their good news of a great joy to all people was taken to other countries, to non-Jews, or gentiles. Very few Jews accepted the belief that in Jesus the Christ, God had made a new covenant with men. In the middle of a tour of persecution of the Christians, Saul of Tarsus was converted and became the great apostle to the gentiles.

This new Christian community wrote down its memories of Jesus the Christ to preserve them for the training of new converts in generations to come. The written records all contained essentially the same good news. The God who had been speaking in all the events of Israel's history and in the prophets had spoken in Jesus.

In his life and message—his teachings about the kingdom and his mighty deeds of healing—Jesus had shown the people what

God's rule in the hearts of men is like. It is like the steadfast love of the father who welcomes home a lost son. It is like the joy of a shepherd who goes out to look for his lost sheep and brings it home, rejoicing.

Keeping the law, Jesus had said, was not a way to prove one's goodness and merit God's approval. The law was to guide men to love God and show this love by concern for their fellowmen. Only God could give this inner attitude of the heart—this love. Men might receive it when they turned to him, repenting of their sin and trusting in his love. Far better to be like the publican who prayed for God's forgiveness because he had not kept all the law, than like the Pharisee who thanked God he was so much better than other men because he had kept all the fine points of the law. The publican would know God's forgiveness and love; the Pharisee would not.

Life was to be lived in trust in God and love for one's fellowmen. This was the fulfillment of the old law and the substance of the new. And God had now made it possible for men to live this way. This was the good news of a great joy.

Jesus had revealed God in the kind of life the prophets had been talking about for centuries: the life of a man who gave himself fully to doing God's will. His teaching, his healing, the kind of person he was—all spoke for God and revealed the love and mercy which were God himself. In Jesus' death, men saw that God gave himself completely to show his love for man even when man was doing his worst evil. In Jesus' resurrection, men learned that God is more powerful than the worst things man can do to deny God's love: God's love will overcome evil and death. In the presence of the Risen Christ and the Spirit he sent, God is still among his people, working out his purpose for them. His steadfast love is present forever and forever. He has written the new covenant on men's hearts.

At his last meal with his disciples Jesus signed and sealed this new covenant. It had been their custom to eat meals together. Sharing a basic necessity such as food and drink meant that a close bond existed between those who broke bread together and drank from the same cup.

After the supper Jesus made this bond of fellowship even stronger and more lasting. He made it the ceremony of the covenant—the *new* covenant by which God was calling together a *new* people. Jesus himself was the sacrifice; his death was the means by which God's kingdom and reign of love would be made known to men. The wine in the cup stood for the pouring out of his blood; the breaking of the bread stood for his body. Gladly he gave his life to show men the love of God.

The apostle Matthew records the giving of the new covenant in this way:

> Now as they were eating, Jesus took bread, and blessed, and broke it, and gave it to the disciples and said, "Take, eat; this is my body." And he took a cup, and when he had given thanks he gave it to them, saying, "Drink of it, all of you; for this is my blood of the covenant, which is poured out for many for the forgiveness of sins."
>
> —*Matthew 26:26–28*

And the apostle Paul, writing to the church he had established at Corinth, said:

> The Lord Jesus on the night when he was betrayed took bread, and when he had given thanks, he broke it, and said, "This is my body which is broken for you. Do this in remembrance of me." In the same way also the cup, after supper, saying, "This cup is the new covenant in my blood. Do this, as often as you drink it, in remembrance of me. For as often as you eat this bread and drink the cup, you proclaim the Lord's death until he comes."
>
> —*1 Corinthians 11:23b–26*

When God saved his people by leading them out of slavery in Egypt, Moses threw the blood of a sacrificial animal upon the altar and the people as the symbol of the covenant sealed between God and men. In the life and death of Jesus Christ, God showed men his love and saved them from slavery to their own pride and willful selfishness. The new covenant was sealed in the outpouring of Christ's life and love represented by the cup and the bread. When Christian people drink of the cup and eat the bread, they express their continuing desire to receive a new heart and belong to the new covenant people of God.

"THAT CHRIST
MAY DWELL
IN YOUR HEARTS
THROUGH FAITH"

The new good news of the covenant was carried from city to city across the Roman Empire. Jewish synagogues became Christian churches. New communities of believers met in homes. A Roman centurion in one city gathered together his neighbors to hear the glad tidings that "in every nation any one who fears him [God] and does what is right is acceptable to him." (Acts 10:35)

The apostle Paul went from place to place as an ambassador of Christ. He organized churches, trained their leaders, and then moved on to new territory. He often wrote letters to help these new churches deal with their problems. He explained more fully what belonging to this new community of faith meant. He expressed the new good news in many ways, according to the needs of the church to which his letter was addressed.

"If any one is in Christ," he told the church at Corinth, "he is a new creation; the old has passed away, behold, the new has come. . . . God was in Christ reconciling the world to himself, not counting their trespasses against them." (2 Corinthians 5:17, 19)

God has offered to all men his forgiving love in Jesus Christ. Those who want God's forgiveness must take the next step. They must respond in faith to the news of God's deed in Christ. Then they become changed, transformed, new persons. Once that happens, nothing can take away the joy and power of being in right relationship with God. Paul wrote to the church at Rome:

Who shall separate us from the love of Christ? Shall tribulation, or distress, or persecution, or famine, or nakedness, or peril, or sword? . . . No, in all these things we are more than conquerors through him who loved us. For I am sure that neither death, nor life, nor angels, nor principalities, nor things present, nor things to come, nor powers, nor height, nor depth, nor anything else in all creation, will be able to separate us from the love of God in Christ Jesus our Lord.

—*Romans 8:35–39*

When the Christians at Corinth were having differences of opinion, Paul wrote that belonging to the new covenant community was like being part of a body. Every part of the body belongs to the others; the body cannot function well unless all its parts work together for the common good.

71

Roman road near Antioch in Syria

If one member suffers, all suffer together; if one member is honored, all rejoice together. . . . Just as the body is one and has many members, and all the members of the body, though many, are one body, so it is with Christ. For by one Spirit we were all baptized into one body—Jews or Greeks, slaves or free—and all were made to drink of one Spirit. . . . Now you are the body of Christ.

—1 Corinthians 12:26, 12–13, 27

Members of the new covenant community will bear witness to God's love in Christ by the way they conduct themselves. Paul wrote to the church at Rome:

Let love be genuine; hate what is evil, hold fast to what is good; love one another with brotherly affection; outdo one another in showing honor. Never flag in zeal, be aglow with the Spirit, serve the Lord. Rejoice in your hope, be patient in tribulation, be constant in prayer. Contribute to the needs of the saints, practice hospitality.

Bless those who persecute you; bless and do not curse them. Rejoice with those who rejoice; weep with those who weep. Live in harmony with one another; . . . Repay no one evil for evil, . . . Do not be overcome by evil, but overcome evil with good.

Owe no one anything, except to love one another; for he who loves his neighbor has fulfilled the law.

—Romans 12:9–21; 13:8

In a letter to the church at Ephesus (ĕf′ ĕ-sŭs), an apostle prayed that God would make the church members ready to be filled with the Spirit of Christ, so that all might be one body in him:

I bow my knees before the Father, from whom every family in heaven and on earth is named, that according to the riches of his glory he may grant you to be strengthened with might through his Spirit in the inner man, and that Christ may dwell in your hearts through faith; that you, being rooted and grounded in love, may have power to comprehend with all the saints what is the breadth and length and height and depth, and to know the love of Christ which surpasses knowledge, that you may be filled with all the fulness of God.

—Ephesians 3:14–19

When the young churches grew a little older, they began to face persecution from the Roman world. These Christians insisted on worshiping an invisible God whom they knew in a Savior called Jesus Christ. They refused to glorify the emperor or bow down before images. The Roman emperor, who wanted to be called divine, began to persecute the stubborn Christians. But bearing suffering bravely, wrote an apostle, was their glory:

> If when you do right and suffer for it you take it patiently, you have God's approval. For to this you have been called, because Christ also suffered for you, leaving you an example, that you should follow in his steps. . . . He himself bore our sins in his body on the tree, that we might die to sin and live to righteousness. By his wounds you have been healed. For you were straying like sheep, but have now returned to the Shepherd and Guardian of your souls.
>
> —*1 Peter 2:20–25*

The new community of the covenant was being called to be a suffering servant of the Lord, as Isaiah of the Exile had seen, just as it was the community of the covenant written upon the heart. And why not? Could there be any greater calling, any more glorious task, for the people of the new covenant?

> You are a chosen race, a royal priesthood, a holy nation, God's own people, that you may declare the wonderful deeds of him who called you out of darkness into his marvelous light.
>
> —*1 Peter 2:9*

CHRIST IN GLORY, tapestry designed by Graham Sutherland, Coventry Cathedral, England

"AND HE SHALL REIGN FOREVER AND EVER"

Persecution descended upon the Christian community with wild fury when the Roman emperor finally declared himself a god. The edict read: Bow before him—or be thrown to the lions and killed. Members of the church needed encouragement to stand fast in their faith. One follower of Christ already had been imprisoned for his faith on a lonely island. He wrote a code message to the churches of Asia Minor. Confidently he assured them that God still ruled, and would rule forever. The beast of the empire might seem to reign triumphant now, but his end would come. God in Christ would conquer evil and death completely, and all the world would bow before him. John, the prisoner, saw in a vision what this victory of faith would be like:

> I looked, and behold, a great multitude which no man could number, from every nation, from all tribes and peoples and tongues, standing before the throne . . . and crying out with a loud voice, "Salvation belongs to our God who sits upon the throne, and to the Lamb [the Christ]! . . . Amen! Blessing and glory and wisdom and thanksgiving and honor and power and might be to our God for ever and ever! Amen."

> Then I heard what seemed to be the voice of a great multitude, like the sound of many waters and like the sound of mighty thunderpeals, crying,
> "Hallelujah! For the Lord our God the Almighty reigns.
> Let us rejoice and exult and give him the glory."

> Then I saw a new heaven and a new earth; for the first heaven and the first earth had passed away, and the sea was no more. And I saw the holy city, new Jerusalem, coming down out of heaven from God, . . . and I heard a great voice . . . saying, "Behold, the dwelling of God is with men. He will dwell with them, and they shall be his people, and God himself will be with them; he will wipe away every tear from their eyes, and death shall be no more, neither shall there be mourning nor crying nor pain any more, for the former things have passed away."

> And I saw no temple in the city, for its temple is the Lord God the Almighty and the Lamb. And the city has no need of sun or moon to shine upon it, for the glory of God is its light, and its lamp is the Lamb. By its light shall the nations walk; and the kings of the earth shall bring their glory into it.
> —*Revelation 7:9–12; 19:6–7a; 21:1–4, 22–24*

Of the kingdom of the Lord there would be no end, for he "shall reign forever and ever."

HERE THE STORY TOOK PLACE

Reading "Our Story" brings us face to face with names of many different places—different because there is a large variety of them, and different because, in many cases, they are names seldom heard today. The names of many of the countries and empires have not appeared on world maps for fifteen hundred years or more. Yet their influence still affects our lives.

Our story began in the ancient Near East in what we now call the Arab world. It started in the land of Egyptian and Semitic empires. Gradually it spread its locale to the Aryan land of Persia and the area occupied today by Turkey. The climax of our story was played out in the Greek and Roman worlds. Then it spread to European territory and in time made its way around the entire world.

Our faces change with age and passing time. It has been the same with the face—the map—of the Middle East. In this map story of the life of the Middle East, you will be able to locate the periods of history and the empires and places mentioned in our story.

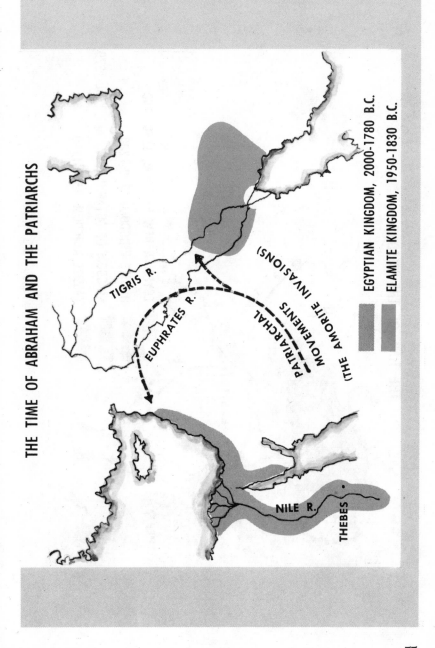

THE TIME OF ABRAHAM AND THE PATRIARCHS

TIGRIS R.

EUPHRATES R.

PATRIARCHAL MOVEMENTS
(THE AMORITE INVASIONS)

NILE R.

THEBES

EGYPTIAN KINGDOM, 2000-1780 B.C.

ELAMITE KINGDOM, 1950-1830 B.C.

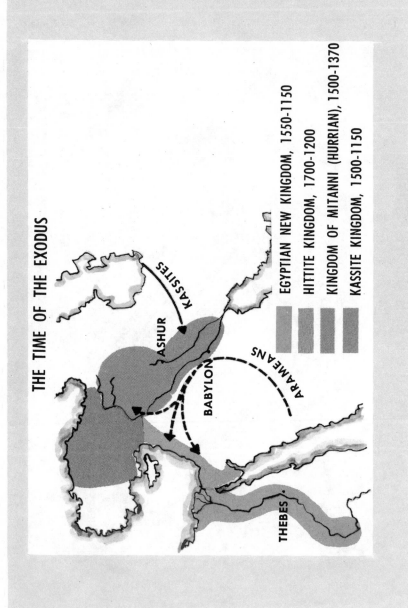

THE TIME OF THE EXODUS

KASSITES

ASHUR

ARAMEANS

BABYLON

THEBES

EGYPTIAN NEW KINGDOM, 1550-1150

HITTITE KINGDOM, 1700-1200

KINGDOM OF MITANNI (HURRIAN), 1500-1370

KASSITE KINGDOM, 1500-1150

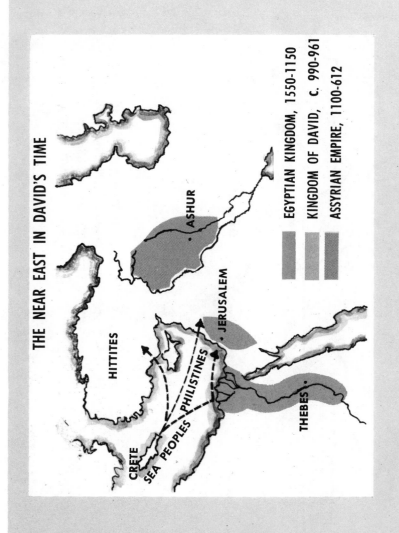

THE NEAR EAST IN DAVID'S TIME

HITTITES

CRETE

SEA PEOPLES

PHILISTINES

• JERUSALEM

ASHUR

THEBES •

EGYPTIAN KINGDOM, 1550-1150

KINGDOM OF DAVID, c. 990-961

ASSYRIAN EMPIRE, 1100-612

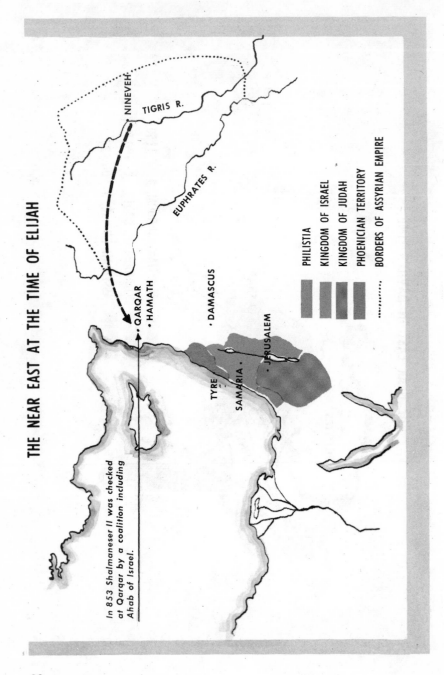

THE NEAR EAST AT THE TIME OF ELIJAH

NINEVEH

TIGRIS R.

EUPHRATES R.

QARQAR
• HAMATH

• DAMASCUS

TYRE

SAMARIA •

JERUSALEM

PHILISTIA

KINGDOM OF ISRAEL

KINGDOM OF JUDAH

PHOENICIAN TERRITORY

BORDERS OF ASSYRIAN EMPIRE

In 853 Shalmaneser II was checked at Qarqar by a coalition including Ahab of Israel.

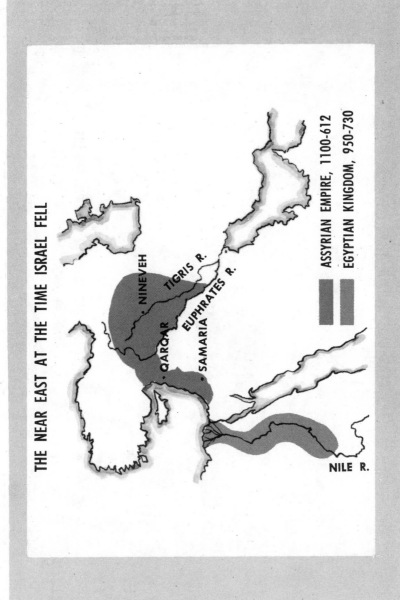

THE NEAR EAST AT THE TIME ISRAEL FELL

NINEVEH

TIGRIS R.

EUPHRATES R.

QARQAR

SAMARIA

NILE R.

ASSYRIAN EMPIRE, 1100-612

EGYPTIAN KINGDOM, 950-730

81

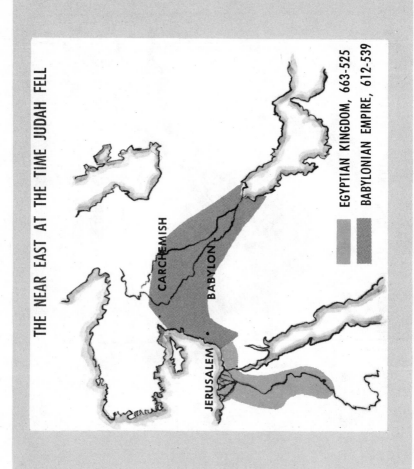

THE NEAR EAST AT THE TIME JUDAH FELL

CARCHEMISH

BABYLON

JERUSALEM

EGYPTIAN KINGDOM, 663-525

BABYLONIAN EMPIRE, 612-539

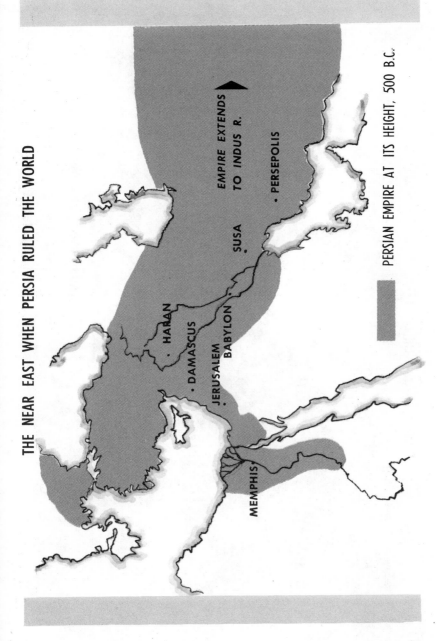

THE NEAR EAST WHEN PERSIA RULED THE WORLD

HARAN

DAMASCUS

JERUSALEM

BABYLON

MEMPHIS

SUSA

EMPIRE EXTENDS
TO INDUS R.

PERSEPOLIS

PERSIAN EMPIRE AT ITS HEIGHT, 500 B.C.

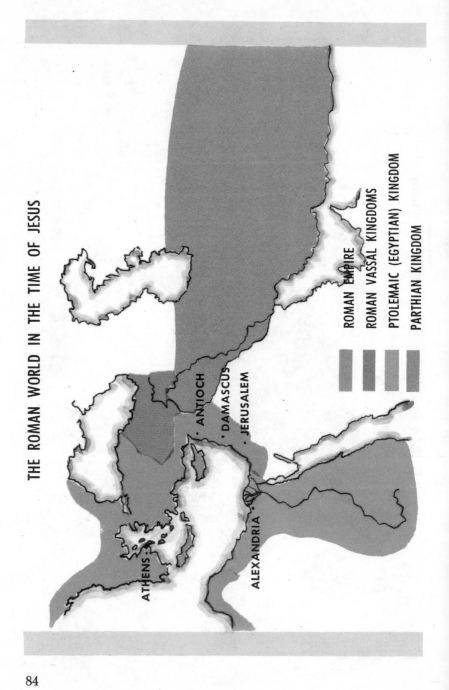

THE ROMAN WORLD IN THE TIME OF JESUS

ATHENS

ALEXANDRIA

ANTIOCH

DAMASCUS

JERUSALEM

ROMAN EMPIRE

ROMAN VASSAL KINGDOMS

PTOLEMAIC (EGYPTIAN) KINGDOM

PARTHIAN KINGDOM

THE ROMAN WORLD WHEN CHRISTIAN CHURCHES WERE VERY YOUNG

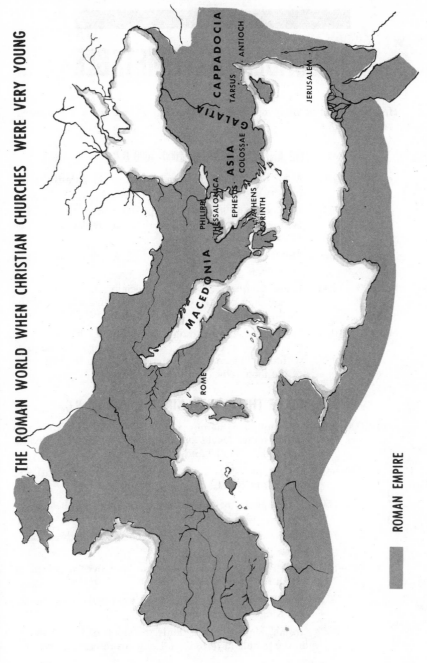

ROMAN EMPIRE

A CONDENSED TIMETABLE

Here is a chart of what took place in "Our Story" and when it happened. (c. means "about")

THE ANCIENT WORLD, 2000–1000 B.C.

c. 2000–1700 Abraham and the patriarchs wander in Palestine's hill country and the Negeb.

c. 1700 Jacob's family moves to Egypt, beginning the period of Hebrew settlement in the northeastern region of the Nile River delta.

c. 1290 or later Moses leads the Hebrews out of Egypt. Ramses II is pharaoh, c. 1290–1224.

c. 1250–1200 Israel conquers Palestine, especially the cities of the central hill country (Bethel, etc.) and Hazor in the north.

c. 1200–1020 The period of the judges in Palestine, including the great battle in Megiddo (Deborah's song), the struggle with the Philistines, and Samuel, Saul, and the beginning of the monarchy (c. 1050–1000).

THE PERIOD OF THE HEBREW KINGS, c. 1000–587 B.C.

c. 1000–922 The united monarchy when Judah and Israel are one nation under David and Solomon. The kingdom divides into Judah (south) and Israel (north) c. 922.

c. 869–849 Elijah speaks for God during the reigns of Ahab and Azariah in Israel.

c. 750 Amos speaks for God during the reign of Jeroboam II in Israel (786–746).

c. 745–737 Hosea speaks for God during the reigns of three minor kings of Israel.

c. 742–700 Isaiah of Jerusalem speaks for God over a period of about forty years.

721 Samaria, capital of Israel, falls to Assyria. The Northern Kingdom ceases to be.

622 Josiah, king of Judah, finds the Book of the Covenant in the temple in Jerusalem. Religious reform follows.

c. 612–580   Jeremiah speaks for God during the reigns of several kings.

598   The first deportation of Jerusalem's leaders to Babylon, Ezekiel among them.

587   Jerusalem falls to Babylonia and the Southern Kingdom ceases to be independent. Many more people are taken into exile.

THE PERIOD OF THE EXILE AND AFTERWARDS, 587–333 B.C.

587 and after   Jerusalem is destroyed and the Babylonian exile begins. Babylon rules Judah as a province.

c. 538   Cyrus of Persia permits the exiles to return to Judah. Near the time of release, Isaiah of the Exile hails Cyrus as God's agent for the restoration of his people.

Between 458 and 398   Ezra returns to reestablish the law and renew the covenant with the people. (Date disputed.)

THE PERIOD UNDER GREEK RULE, 333–63 B.C. (INTERTESTAMENTAL PERIOD)

c. 336–323   Alexander the Great of Greece extends his empire to India and Egypt.

198   Syria (Seleucid empire) seizes control of Palestine. In 167 B.C. the Jews, led by the Maccabees, revolt against Syria.

63   Rome seizes control of Palestine.

THE PERIOD UNDER ROMAN RULE, 63 B.C. TO A.D. 325

31 B.C.–A.D. 14   Augustus is emperor of Rome.

6 or 4 B.C.–A.D. 29   The birth and ministry of Jesus.

A.D. 32–62   Paul leads the missionary expansion of the church.

A.D. 54–68   Nero rules Rome. In A.D. 64 the city burns and the Christians there are persecuted.

A.D. 66–70   Jews revolt. Jerusalem is destroyed A.D. 70.

A.D. 90 and after   More persecutions of the Christians in the empire.

SOME THINGS WE HAVE FOUND

As you have discovered, the Bible is the story of a people who lived at a certain time and place, and who interpreted what happened to them as taking place under God's guiding hand. For many years the biblical story was accepted at literal face value. Everything in it was thought to have happened *exactly* as described. Then came a period when some people doubted that very much of it, particularly what happened before the times of the Old Testament prophets, was based on historical fact or life in historical times.

In recent years, however, archaeologists have made many discoveries in the Middle East which shed considerable light on what the Bible relates. People like Abraham and the patriarchs did migrate from east to west. An invasion that destroyed many cities in central Palestine did occur in the thirteenth century B.C. Fertility gods were worshiped throughout the ancient Near East, and we have found a whole library of Syrian songs about Baal and his fellow gods. The picture stories that follow tell about a very few of the many archaeological findings which have helped bring the biblical story—our story—to life.

Statue of Lamgi-Mari, king of Mari

IN THE
LAND OF ABRAHAM

THE CITY OF MARI

In 1933 the little town of Abu Kemal on the flat Euphrates River plain lay wilting in the heat of summer. The lieutenant of this Syrian mandate sat dozing in his chair. He stirred regretfully when a commotion broke out in the hall near his door. Another Arab quarrel to settle, no doubt. The lieutenant yawned, got up, and went outside. Arabs were there, all right, and they were gesturing excitedly. But it was not a quarrel. Streams of language nearly drowned the lieutenant, but finally the interpreter got it all straight.

The people had been burying a relative on a hillside near the town. They were just digging the grave when a spade threw out a stone figure that looked almost like a corpse!

That stone figure brought a sudden flood of visitors and archaeologists to sleepy little Abu Kemal.

An ancient city lay beneath the mound where the grave had been dug. It proved to be Mari (mä′ rē), royal city of the kingdom of Mari which ruled this area during the period when Abraham might have been wandering from Haran to the promised new land.

Inhabitants of Mari were peace-loving people. All their figures and statues bear cheerful faces. One of the first great finds was the figure of Lamgi-Mari, king of Mari. On his right shoulder were carved these words: "I am Lamgi-Mari . . . king . . . of . . . Mari . . . the great . . . Issakkv . . . who worships his statue . . . of Ishtar." There is a pleasant, almost perky look on the face of this ancient ruler.

Most exciting of the discoveries at Mari was the palace of Zimri-Lim, last king of the nation. Even though soldiers of Hammurabi of old Babylon burned the palace when they conquered Mari about 1700 B.C., much of it escaped destruction. The massive walls are

Fresco from the walls of the palace of Zimri-Lin, Mari

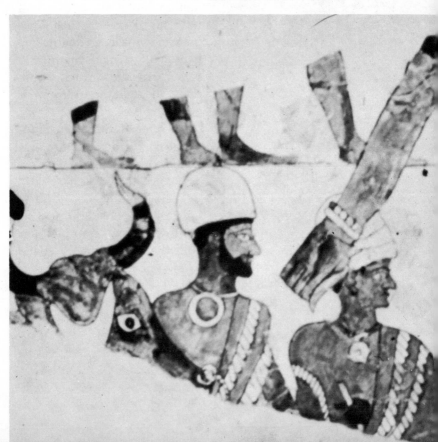

still sixteen feet high. Delicate frescoes which ornamented them have been unearthed. The colors of these oldest paintings in Mesopotamia still seem so brilliant that they might have been painted yesterday.

Thousands of tablets from the palace archives record business transactions and give us a picture of life among this people. Names familiar to us in the Bible appear in these court records. Benjamin was the name given to a group of frontier villages—and Benjamin is the name of a tribe of Israel. Names like Peleg, Serug, Nahor, and Terah (the names of Abraham's forefathers), and Haran (the city to which Terah moved after leaving Ur) appear in the Mari tablets as the names of cities in the Padan-Aram (pā′ dăn-ā′ răm) plain in the land of Mari. Jacob returned to this country to seek a wife because from it his forefather Abraham had come.

The patriarchal past unrolls before us today when we look at the ruins of Mari.

Storm-god Baal from Arslân-Tash.
Similar figures were found at Ras Shamra

IN THE
LANDS OF BAAL

WORSHIP AT RAS SHAMRA

Some of the charges leveled against Israel by the prophets may shock us. Hosea said Israel had acted like a harlot by running after Baal and the Canaanite gods. Isaiah of Jerusalem said the city of Zion had become a harlot. Jeremiah denounced the people for worshiping poles and running after other gods under every tree and on every high place. The prophets never minced words when condemning Baal worship.

In the past, people have said the Bible overdoes its descriptions of Baal worship. But archaeology recently has found many records of Canaanite religion which show that the prophets' charges were based on actual religious practices. Canaanite religion was very different from Israel's worship. It affected the political, social, and moral life of the country. A real choice was necessary.

Discoveries at Ras Shamra (räs shäm' rà) on the coast of Syria opposite Cyprus give us a better understanding of the positive and negative aspects of Canaanite religion. In the 1920's a peasant was plowing his field near the shore when his plow cut into a long underground passage. It led to a tomb. Archaeologists grew excited when they heard the report and flocked to the scene. Half a mile from the shore a rounded, artificial hill rose. Such round hills always spell adventure for archaeologists. They often prove to be "mounds," the buried ruins of cities or temples. This hill in Syria, named Ras Shamra, turned out to be such a mound: the remains of the ancient Phoenician royal city of Ugarit (ū' gà-rĭt).

Two temples crowned the site. One was dedicated to Baal and the other to Dagon, another of the Canaanite gods. Between the temples stood houses of rich merchants and—most valuable find of all—the library of the high priest of Ugarit. Thousands of tablets recorded the myths and worship practices of the religions of the Canaanite peoples, the

Figure of fertility goddess found at Ras Shamra

93

Terracotta statues of goddess of fertility, found
throughout Palestine

very religions Israel encountered in the midst of the Promised
Land.

The rites were primitive and sensual, especially those customs
related to worship of the fertility goddess. Worshipers used magic
in its worst possible forms: engaging in the forms of human propa-
gation and sexual relations as imitative magic to produce the rains
on which life in agricultural Canaan depended. Canaanite religion
even made use of sacred prostitution to this end. Charms and

amulets were used also as aids in ensuring the recurrence of the fertility cycle in nature.

The gods and goddesses were often bloodthirsty and ferocious. Anath (ā' năth), sister and wife of Baal and goddess of war, took delight in wading in blood up to her knees. Astarte (ăs-tär' tē), goddess of fertility, also known as Ashtoreth (ăsh' tŏ-rĕth), wore a snake around her neck to symbolize fertility. Poles were erected near her altars. When we read in Kings that the people of Israel built "high places, and pillars, and Asherim on every high hill and under every green tree," we know how deeply Baalism threatened worship of the true God. (1 Kings 14:23)

Hundreds of hymns and songs were found in the library at Ras Shamra. In form, they are often similar to the psalms, but the content is very different. Here is a brief sample taken from the myth of Baal and Anath, the dying and rising god who must be returned to life before the rains can come:

'Let the heavens rain oil
The wadies run with honey
That I may know that Aliyn Baal is alive
That the Prince, Lord of Earth, exists.'

Ltpn, God of Mercy, rejoices.
His feet he sets on the footstool
He cracks a smile and laughs.
He lifts his voice
And shouts:
'Let me sit and rest
And let my soul repose in my breast
For Aliyn Baal is alive
For the Prince, Lord of Earth, exists.' [1]

Many scholars believe that Psalm 29 was originally a Canaanite psalm which Yahweh worshipers borrowed and used for Yahweh. Its nature imagery of thunder and storm is typical of Canaanite hymns found at Ras Shamra. This kind of poetry had a profound influence on Hebrew psalmody, just as the entire Canaanite religion affected Israelite architecture, worship, and everyday life. The discovery at Ras Shamra makes this very clear.

Panorama of the ruins of Ephesus, theater in the foreground

IN THE LANDS
OF PAUL'S PREACHING

"GREAT IS ARTEMIS
OF THE EPHESIANS"

"CHRISTIAN MINISTER'S PREACHING IRES BUSINESS LEADERS! THOUSANDS RIOT!" Such a headline would make us do a quick double take today, and even then we would probably think that someone had gone out of his mind to dream it up. Most preaching, in America at least, doesn't make such an impact on the public.

But the headline is not fiction. It describes a real event which occurred in New Testament times in the city of Ephesus. Chapter 19 of the book of Acts furnishes details, and once again, archaeological discoveries have testified to the Bible story by unearthing ruins of the city.

The ancient city of Ephesus was located in what is now Turkey. In Paul's time it was a rich trading port and the center for the worship of Artemis (är′ tĕ-mĭs), or Diana, the mother goddess whom, according to her followers, "all Asia and the world worship." Hers was a fertility cult, with worship customs similar to those of the Baals in Canaanite times.

Into this important city came Paul, preaching Jesus Christ and denouncing worship of statuettes of Diana. His preaching was effective. Many were converted, so many, in fact, that sale of silver statuettes fell off. The profitable business of making these images was undermined; the silversmiths were alarmed. One of them, Demetrius (dĕ-mē′ trĭ-ŭs) by name, stirred up a crowd of fellow silversmiths and other citizens. They all assembled in the big municipal theater which overlooked the city from the slope of Mt. Pion. Paul was expected to preach there, and when some of his followers arrived, the crowd rioted against them. For two hours the mob shouted, "Great is Artemis of the Ephesians!" Finally city officials quieted the shrieking. In the meantime Paul's friends had managed to restrain him from heading straight for the theater to face his opponents.

Not only the theater, which seated almost 25,000 people, but most of the main buildings of ancient Ephesus have been unearthed. The marketplace, or forum, can be seen. So can the ruins of the magnificent main street, the Arkadiane, which ran for a third of a mile from the theater to the harbor. Paved in marble, it was lined all the way with an exquisite colonnade and shops.

Most impressive of all, perhaps, are the ruins of the great temple to Diana. It was one of the seven wonders of the ancient world. Legends of its magnificence have come down through history. However, it took a long time for people to find its ruins. Finally it was located by J. T. Wood, an English architect who spent six years in searching. Month after month he dug here and there in the ruins of the city, but no part of a temple appeared. One day, however, he uncovered a signpost in the theater. At last, a clue! The sign described the route along which statues of Diana would be carried from the temple to the theater on her birthday.

The excited architect followed the directions exactly as given.

A Roman copy from the
third century after Christ
of a statue of Diana of Ephesus

They led him to a mound northeast of the city. Down through twenty-five feet of soil and debris he and his co-workers dug, inch by inch. At last they found it! Ruins of a splendid pavement, bases of massive pillars, remains of sculptures, and fragments of a huge altar were uncovered. It was the temple of Diana. The platform was about 239 feet wide and 418 feet long. The temple building itself had been about 160 feet wide, 340 feet long, with 100 columns 55 feet high. Foundations of the altar were 20 feet square.

To make the Bible story even more real, thirty-five years later another archaeologist found silver, gold, bronze, and ivory statues of Diana under the ruins of the altar. Who knows? Perhaps some in that collection may have been made by the very craftsmen who rioted against Paul's preaching.

NEGRO SPIRITUALS
THAT HELP TELL THE STORY

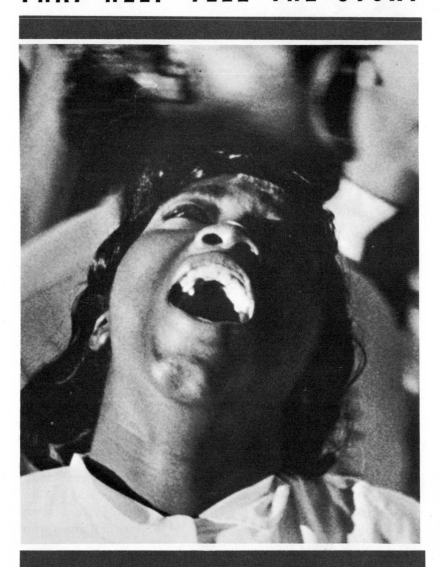

Go Down, Moses

Negro Spiritual

GO DOWN MOSES *Irregular*
Negro Melody

1 When Is - rael was in E-gypt's land,
2 Thus saith the Lord, bold Mo - ses said, Let my peo - ple go,
3 No more in bond-age shall they toil,

Op-pressed so hard they could not stand,
If not I'll smite your first-born dead, Let my peo - ple go.
Let them come out with E - gypt's spoil,

REFRAIN

Go down, Mo - ses, 'Way down in E-gypt's land,

Tell old Phar - aoh, To let my peo-ple go.

Music from *American Negro Songs and Spirituals* by John W. Work. Copyright 1940 by John W. Work. Used by permission of Crown Publishers, Inc.

Deep River

Deep   riv - er, my home is o - ver Jor - dan,
Deep, deep

Fine

Deep   riv - er, Lord, I want to cross o - ver in - to camp-ground.
Deep, deep

O don't you want to   go   to that gos - pel feast, That

prom - ised land where all   is   peace, O don't you want to

D.C.

go to that prom - ised land, that land   where all is peace?

Arr. Copyright in "Southland Spirituals" by Homer Rodeheaver, Used by permission.

There Is a Balm in Gilead

Spiritual

Arr. by Francis Ames
Harm. by Frank A. McConnell

There is a balm in Gil - e - ad To make the wound-ed whole. There is a

balm in Gil - e - ad To heal the sin-sick soul. There is a soul. Some-
Don't
You

times I feel dis-cour-aged and think my work in vain, But then the Ho-ly
ev - er feel dis-cour-aged, our Fa-ther is our Friend, And if you lack for
may not preach like Pe-ter, you may not pray like Paul, But you can tell the

Spir - it re-vives my soul a - gain.
knowl-edge He'll not re-fuse to lend. There is a balm in Gil - e - ad To
sto - ry of One who died for all.

make the wound-ed whole. There is a balm in Gil - e - ad To heal the sin-sick soul.

From *Sing to the Lord*. The Christian Education Press, 1959. Used by permission.

Go, Tell It on the Mountain

Negro Spiritual

GO TELL IT ON THE MOUNTAIN *Irregular*
Negro Melody

REFRAIN

Go, tell it on the moun - tain, O - ver the hills and ev - ery-where;

Go, tell it on the moun - tain That Je - sus Christ is born!

1 While shep-herds kept their watch-ing O'er si - lent flocks by night, Be -
2 The shep-herds feared and trem-bled When lo! a - bove the earth Rang
3 Down in a low - ly man - ger The hum-ble Christ was born, And

hold through-out the heav - ens There shone a ho - ly light.
out the an - gel cho - rus That hailed our Sav - ior's birth.
God sent us sal - va - tion That bless - ed Christ-mas morn.

From *American Negro Songs and Spirituals* by John W. Work. Copyright 1940 by John W. Work. Used by permission of Crown Publishers, Inc.

Let Us Break Bread Together

Negro Spiritual

LET US BREAK BREAD 7.3.7.3. *with Refrain*
Negro Melody

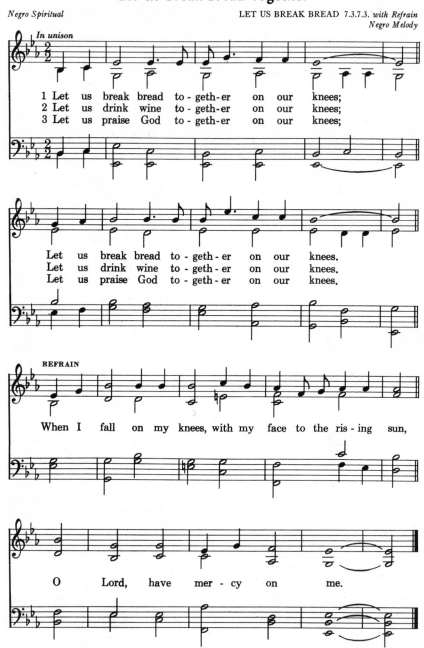

1 Let us break bread to-geth-er on our knees;
2 Let us drink wine to-geth-er on our knees;
3 Let us praise God to-geth-er on our knees;

Let us break bread to-geth-er on our knees.
Let us drink wine to-geth-er on our knees.
Let us praise God to-geth-er on our knees.

REFRAIN

When I fall on my knees, with my face to the ris-ing sun,

O Lord, have mer-cy on me.

He Is King of Kings

Spiritual

Arr. by Olive J. Williams
Harm. by Frank A. McConnell

REFRAIN

He is King of Kings. He is Lord of Lords.

Je - sus Christ the first and last, No man works like Him,

1. I know that my Re - deem - er lives, No man works like Him,
2. He builds a plat-form in the air, No man works like Him,
3. O sin - ner if you will be - lieve, No man works like Him,

And by His love sweet bless-ing gives, No man works like Him.
And calls the saints from ev - ery - where, No man works like Him.
Grace of the Lord you will re - ceive, No man works like Him.

From *Sing to the Lord*. The Christian Education Press, 1959. Used by permission.

107

WE DO COVENANT TOGETHER

You have read in the Bible of the covenant between the God of Israel and the people whom he called to serve him in a special way. This covenant is unique; there is no other like it, for it is between God and man. But there have been many covenants between two persons, or between two groups of persons. Here are a few samples of covenants between people which express or contain the quality of covenant relationship.

THE SALEM CHURCH COVENANT, 1629

We covenant with the Lord and one with an other and doe bynd our selves in the presence of God, to walke together in all his waies, according as he is pleased to reveale himself unto us in his blessed word of truth.

THE MAYFLOWER COMPACT

In ye name of God Amen. We whose names are underwriten, the loyall subjects of our dread soveraigne lord King James, by ye grace of God, of Great Britaine, Franc & Ireland king, defender of ye faith, &c.

Haveing undertaken, for ye glorie of God, and advancemente of ye christian faith and honour of our king & countrie, a voyage to plant ye first colonie in ye Northerne parts of Virginia. Doe by these presents solemnly & mutualy in ye presence of God, and one of another; covenant & combine our selves togeather into a civill body politick; for our better ordering, & preservation & furtherance of ye ends aforesaid; and by vertue hearof to enacte, constitute, and frame shuch just & equall lawes, ordinances, Acts, constitutions, & offices, from time to time, as shall be thought most meete & convenient for ye generall good of ye Colonie: unto which we promise all due submission and obedience. In witness whereof we have hereunder subscribed our names at Cap-Codd ye .11. of November, in ye year of ye raigne of our soveraigne lord king James of England, France & Ireland ye eighteenth and of Scotland ye fiftie fourth. Ano Dom. 1620.

THE PREAMBLE OF THE COVENANT OF THE LEAGUE OF NATIONS

THE HIGH CONTRACTING PARTIES

In order to promote international co-operation and to achieve international peace and security

by the acceptance of obligations not to resort to war,

by the prescription of open, just and honourable relations between nations,

by the firm establishment of the understandings of international law as
the actual rule of conduct among Governments,
and by the maintenance of justice and scrupulous respect for all treaty
obligations in the dealings of organised peoples with one another,
Agree to this Covenant of the League of Nations.
(*Then follow the various articles of the Covenant itself.*)

THE CHARTER OF THE UNITED NATIONS

In similar *spirit,* this document states the purposes and principles
of the United Nations, and then lists the principles in accordance
with which the organization and its members shall act. Included is:

2. All Members, in order to ensure to all of them the rights and benefits
resulting from membership, shall fulfil in good faith the obligations
assumed by them in accordance with the present charter.

THE MARRIAGE VOWS

I, N_____, take thee, N_____, to be my wedded wife;
and I do promise and covenant, before God and these witnesses, to be thy
loving and faithful husband, in plenty and in want, in joy and in sorrow,
in sickness and in health; as long as we both shall live.

I, N_____, take thee, N_____, to be my wedded husband;
and I do promise and covenant, before God and these witnesses, to be thy loving and faithful wife; in plenty and in want, in joy and in sorrow, in sickness
and in health; as long as we both shall live.[2]

OUR CHURCH OR CLASS COVENANT

ORDER
OF
SERVICE[3]

for such as would enter into or renew their
COVENANT WITH GOD
*for use on the first Sunday of the year
or other occasion*

The Church of South India

Come, Let Us Use the Grace Divine (*tune: Dundee*)

> Come, let us use the grace divine,
> And all, with one accord,
> In a perpetual covenant join
> Ourselves to Christ the Lord:
>
> Give up ourselves, through Jesus' power,
> His name to glorify;
> And promise, in this sacred hour,
> For God to live and die.
>
> The covenant we this moment make
> Be ever kept in mind;
> We will no more our God forsake,
> Or cast his words behind.
>
> We never will throw off his fear
> Who hears our solemn vow;
> And if thou art well pleased to hear,
> Come down and meet us now.
>
> To each the covenant blood apply,
> Which takes our sins away;
> And register our names on high,
> And keep us to that day. Amen.

After this the minister says:

Let us pray,

Almighty God, unto whom all hearts be open, all desires known, and from whom no secrets are hid; Cleanse the thoughts of our hearts by the inspiration of thy Holy Spirit, that we may perfectly love thee, and worthily magnify thy holy name; through Christ our Lord. **Amen.**

Then the people sit, and the minister says:

Dearly beloved, the Christian Life, to which we are called, is a life in Christ, redeemed from sin by him and, through him, consecrated to God. Upon this life we have entered, having been admitted into that new covenant of which our Lord Jesus Christ is mediator, and which he sealed with his own blood, that it might stand for ever.

111

On God's part, the covenant is his reconciling of the world to himself in Jesus Christ and his promise that he will fulfil in and through us all that he declared in him, who is the author and perfecter of our faith. That his promise stands we are sure, for we have known his goodness and proved his grace in our lives day by day.

On our part we have received this covenant through faith, and stand pledged to live no more unto ourselves, but unto him who loved us and gave himself for us and has called us to serve him to the praise of his glory.

From time to time we renew our vows of consecration, especially when we gather at the table of the Lord; and on this day we meet expressly, that we may joyfully and solemnly renew the covenant which binds us to God.

Let us then, remembering the mercies of God, and the hope of his calling, lift up our hearts to him in adoration.

ADORATION

Let us pray,
Let us adore the Father, the God of love who created us;
Who every moment preserves and sustains us;
Who has loved us with an everlasting love, and given us the light of the knowledge of his glory in the face of Jesus Christ.

We adore thee, O God, we acknowledge thee to be the Lord.

Let us glory in the grace of our Lord Jesus Christ;
Who, though he was rich, yet for our sakes became poor;
Who went about doing good and preaching the gospel of the kingdom;
Who was tempted in all points like as we are, yet without sin;
Who became obedient unto death, even the death of the cross;
Who was dead and is alive for evermore;
Who has opened the kingdom of heaven to all believers;
Who sitteth at the right hand of God in the glory of the Father;
Who shall come again as judge and king.

Thou art the King of Glory, O Christ.

Let us rejoice in the fellowship of the Holy Spirit, the Lord, the giver of life, by whom we are born into the family of God, and made members of the body of Christ;

Whose witness confirms us;

Whose wisdom teaches us;

Whose power enables us;

Who is ready to do for us exceeding abundantly above all that we ask or think.

All praise to thee, O Holy Spirit.

Here follows a period of silent prayer.

THANKSGIVING

Let us rise and give thanks to God for his manifold mercies.

All stand.

O God our Father, the fountain of all goodness, who hast been gracious to us through all the years of our life: we give thee thanks for thy loving-kindness which has filled our days and brought us to this time and place.

We praise thy Holy Name, O Lord.

Thou hast given us life and reason, and set us in a world which is full of thy glory. Thou hast comforted us with kindred and friends, and ministered to us through the hands and minds of our fellows.

We praise thy Holy Name, O Lord.

Thou has set in our hearts a hunger for thee, and given us thy peace. Thou hast redeemed us and called us with a high calling in Jesus Christ. Thou hast given us a place in the fellowship of thy Spirit and the witness of thy church.

We praise thy Holy Name, O Lord.

In darkness thou hast been our light; in adversity and temptation a rock of strength; in our joys the very crown of joy; in our labours the all-sufficient reward.

We praise thy Holy Name, O Lord.

Thou hast remembered us when we have forgotten thee, followed

113

us even when we fled from thee, met us with forgiveness when we turned back to thee. For all thy long-suffering and the abundance of thy grace.

We praise thy Holy Name, O Lord.

CONFESSION

And now let us examine ourselves, asking God to search our hearts.

Silent confession, all kneeling.

Let us humbly confess our sins to God, lest by self-deceit we shut ourselves out from his presence.

Let us pray,

O God our Father, who hast set forth the way of life for us in thy beloved Son: we confess with shame our slowness to learn of him, our reluctance to follow him. Thou hast spoken and called, and we have not given heed; thy beauty has shone forth and we have been blind; thou hast met us in our neighbour and we have passed by. We have taken great benefits with little thanks; we have been unworthy of thy changeless love.

Have mercy upon us and forgive us, O Lord.

Forgive us, we beseech thee, the poverty of our worship, the formality and selfishness of our prayers, our inconstancy and unbelief, our neglect of fellowship and of the means of grace, our hesitating witness for Christ, our hypocrisy and our wilful ignorance of thy ways.

Have mercy upon us and forgive us, O Lord.

Forgive us wherein we have wasted our time or misused our gifts. Forgive us wherein we have excused our own wrong-doing or evaded our responsibilities. Forgive us that we have been unwilling to overcome evil with good, that we have shrunk from bearing the cross.

Have mercy upon us and forgive us, O Lord.

Forgive us that so little of thy love has reached others through us, and that we have borne so lightly wrongs and sufferings that

114

were not our own. Forgive us wherein we have cherished the things that divide us from others, and wherein we have been thoughtless in our judgements, hasty in condemnation, grudging in forgiveness.

Have mercy upon us and forgive us, O Lord.

If we have made no ventures in fellowship; if we have kept in our heart a grievance against another; if we have not sought reconciliation; if we have been eager for the punishment of wrong-doers, and slow to seek their redemption.

Have mercy upon us and forgive us, O Lord.

Have mercy upon me, O God, according to thy loving-kindness; according to the multitude of thy tender mercies blot out my transgressions. Wash me thoroughly from mine iniquity, and cleanse me from my sin. Create in me a clean heart, O God, and renew a right spirit within me.

Then, the people still kneeling, the minister rises and says:

This is the message which we heard from him, and declare unto you, that God is light, and in him is no darkness at all. If we walk in the light, as he is in the light, we have fellowship one with another, and the blood of Jesus his Son cleanseth us from all sin. If we say that we have no sin, we deceive ourselves, and the truth is not in us. If we confess our sins, he is faithful and righteous to forgive us our sins, and to cleanse us from all unrighteousness.

Amen. Thanks be to God.

The Lord be with you;

And with thy spirit.

Let us pray,

O God, who hast appointed our Lord Jesus Christ as mediator of a new covenant, grant us grace, we beseech thee, to draw near with fullness of faith and join ourselves in a perpetual covenant to thee; through the same Jesus Christ our Lord. **Amen.**

Here all stand, and the lessons are read.

OLD TESTAMENT: Jeremiah 31:31–33
EPISTLE: Hebrews 12:22–25a
GOSPEL: Matthew 11:27–30

All remain standing, and the minister says:

And now, beloved, let us with all our heart renew our part in the covenant that God has made with his people, and take the yoke of Christ upon us.

This taking of his yoke means that we are heartily content that he should appoint us our place and work, and that he alone should be our reward.

Christ has many services to be done; some are easy, others are difficult; some bring honour, others bring reproach; some are suitable to our natural inclinations and temporal interests, others are contrary to both. In some we may please Christ and please ourselves, in others we cannot please Christ except by denying ourselves. Yet the power to do all these things is assuredly given us in Christ, who strengtheneth us.

Therefore let us make the covenant of God our own. Let us engage our heart to the Lord, and resolve in his strength never to go back.

Being thus prepared, let us now, in sincere dependence on his grace and trusting in his promises, yield ourselves anew to him, meekly kneeling upon our knees.

All kneel.

Here the minister says in the name of all:

O Lord God, Holy Father, who hast called us through Christ to be partakers in this gracious covenant, we take upon ourselves with joy the yoke of obedience, and engage ourselves, for love of thee, to seek and do thy perfect will. We are no longer our own, but thine.

Here all the people join:

I am no longer my own, but thine. Put me to what thou wilt, rank me with whom thou wilt; put me to doing, put me to suffering; let me be employed for thee or laid aside for thee, exalted for thee or brought low for thee; let me be full, let me be empty; let me have all things, let me have nothing; I freely and heartily yield all things to thy pleasure and disposal.

And now, O glorious and blessed God, Father, Son, and Holy
Spirit, thou art mine, and I am thine. So be it. And the covenant
which I have made on earth, let it be ratified in heaven. Amen.

Silence.

Then the minister and people rise, and the minister says:
Jesus said: This cup is the new covenant in my blood, even that
which is poured out for you.

Praise be to thee, O Christ.

Behold, how good and joyful a thing it is, brethren, to dwell
together in unity.

*The service of the Lord's supper shall continue from this place.
If this is not convenient, then the service ends as follows:*

Silence after the Covenant

THE LORD'S PRAYER

HYMN OR LYRIC (*during which the offerings are collected*)

DEDICATION OF OFFERING

Glory be to thee, O God the Father, who hast loved us and made
us accepted in thy beloved Son.

Amen. Glory to thee, our Father.

Glory be to thee, O God the Son, who hast loved us and loosed
us from our sins by thine own blood.

Amen. Glory to thee, our Saviour.

Glory be to thee, O God the Holy Spirit, who sheddest the love
of God abroad in our hearts and dost free us from the law of sin
and death.

Amen. Glory to thee, our Guide and Strengthener.

O one true God, Father, Son, and Holy Spirit, to thee be all love
and all glory for time and for eternity.

**Amen. Blessing, and glory, and wisdom, and thanksgiving, and
honour, and power, and might, be unto our God for ever and ever.
Amen.**

PRAYERS
OF THE PEOPLE
OF THE
NEW COVENANT

"I do not pray for these only, but also for those who are to believe in me through their word, that they may all be one; even as thou, Father, art in me, and I in thee, that they also may be in us, so that the world may believe that thou hast sent me. The glory which thou hast given me I have given to them, that they may be one even as we are one, I in them and thou in me, that they may become perfectly one, so that the world may know that thou hast sent me and hast loved them even as thou hast loved me. . . . O righteous Father, the world has not known thee, but I have known thee; and these know that thou hast sent me. I made known to them thy name, and I will make it known, that the love with which thou hast loved me may be in them, and I in them."

—Jesus' prayer in John 17:20–26

For this reason I bow my knees before the Father, from whom every family in heaven and on earth is named, that according to the riches of his glory he may grant you to be strengthened with might through his Spirit in the inner man, and that Christ may dwell in your hearts through faith; that you, being rooted and grounded in love, may have power to comprehend with all the saints what is the breadth and length and height and depth, and to know the love of Christ which surpasses knowledge, that you may be filled with all the fulness of God.

—Ephesians 3:14–19

May the God of steadfastness and encouragement grant you to live in such harmony with one another, in accord with Christ Jesus, that together you may with one voice glorify the God and Father of our Lord Jesus Christ.

—Romans 15:5–6

May the God of hope fill you with all joy and peace in believing, so that by the power of the Holy Spirit you may abound in hope.

—Romans 15:13

Now to him who by the power at work within us is able to do far more abundantly than all that we ask or think, to him be glory in the church and in Christ Jesus to all generations, for ever and ever. Amen.

—Ephesians 3:20–21

The grace of the Lord Jesus Christ and the love of God and the fellowship of the Holy Spirit be with you all.

—2 Corinthians 13:14

Now may our Lord Jesus Christ himself, and God our Father, who loved us and gave us eternal comfort and good hope through grace, comfort your hearts and establish them in every good work and word.

—2 Thessalonians 2:16

Now may the Lord of peace himself give you peace at all times in all ways. The Lord be with you all.

—2 Thessalonians 3:16

Now may the God of peace who brought again from the dead our Lord Jesus, the great shepherd of the sheep, by the blood of the eternal covenant, equip you with everything good that you may do his will, working in you that which is pleasing in his sight, through Jesus Christ; to whom be glory for ever and ever. Amen.

—Hebrews 13:20–21

Now to him who is able to keep you from falling and to present you without blemish before the presence of his glory with rejoicing, to the only God, our Savior through Jesus Christ our Lord, be glory, majesty, dominion, and authority, before all time and now and for ever. Amen.

—Jude 24–25

Grace to you and peace from God our Father and the Lord Jesus Christ.

—Romans 1:7b; Ephesians 1:2;
1 Corinthians 1:3; 2 Corinthians 1:2; Philippians 1:2

"Amen! Blessing and glory and wisdom and thanksgiving and honor and power and might be to our God for ever and ever! Amen."

—Revelation 7:12

"Great and wonderful are thy deeds,
O Lord God the Almighty!
Just and true are thy ways,
O King of the ages!
Who shall not fear and glorify thy name, O Lord?
For thou alone art holy.
All nations shall come and worship thee,
for thy judgments have been revealed."

—Revelation 15:3b–4

"Hallelujah! For the Lord our God the Almighty reigns.
Let us rejoice and exult and give him the glory."

—Revelation 19:6b–7

PRONUNCIATION GUIDE

ă as in sat   ī as in kite
ä as in calm   ŏ as in on
ā as in made   ō as in more
å as in arise   ŭ as in up
ĕ as in set   û as in urge
ē as in meet   ū as in rule
ĭ as in sit

FOOTNOTES

1. Used by permission of Cyrus H. Gordon, translator.
2. From *The Book of Common Worship* (1905, 1906). The Presbyterian Church in the U.S.A. Used by permission.
3. Adapted from the "Covenant Service" in the Book of Offices, Published by the Methodist Publishing House, London (1936). Used by permission of the Methodist Publishing House, London, Oxford University Press, Madras, and the Synod of the Church of South India.

CREDITS

Grateful acknowledgment is due to the following individuals, museums, and photographic services for permission to reproduce their material.

American Archives of World Art, pages 90–91
Anderson-Art Reference Bureau, page 65
Archives Photographiques, Paris, page 92
Trustees of the British Museum, London, page 47
Caisse Nationale des Monuments Historiques, Paris, page 92
Ewing Galloway, pages 5, 96–97
Giraudon, Paris, pages 26, 93
Courtesy of the Oriental Institute, University of Chicago, pages 21, 29, 31
The Matson Photo Service, pages 10, 19, 23, 70
Metropolitan Museum of Art, Gift of John D. Rockefeller, Jr., 1932, page 34
Courtesy of the Oriental Institute, University of Chicago, pages 51, 53 (Painting by M. Bardin after Unger)
Courtesy of American Schools of Oriental Research, photograph by John Trever, page 59
Palestine Archaeological Museum, Jerusalem, Jordan, cover, pages 39, 55, 94
James B. Pritchard, page 89
Superintendent of Antiquities of Campania-Naples, page 99
Kenneth Thompson, pages 100, 104
P. W. & L. Thompson Ltd., Coventry, page 74
John Trever, page 59
University Museum, University of Pennsylvania, page 89
Willem van de Poll, Amsterdam, pages 14–15
Edward Wallowitch, page 118

The maps on pages 77–85 were drawn by Art Wood.